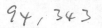

Employment for
DISABLED
PEOPLE

Employment for DISABLED PEOPLE

Mary Thompson

Kogan Page

First published in Great Britain in 1986
by Kogan Page Limited, 120 Pentonville Road,
London N1 9JN

British Library Cataloguing in Publication Data

Thompson, Mary
    Employment for disabled people.
    1. Physically handicapped — Employment —
    Great Britain
    I. Title
    331.5'9   HD7256.G7

    ISBN 1-85091-127-4

Printed and bound in Great Britain by
Billing & Sons Ltd, Worcester

Contents

Introduction

I have written this book for disabled people and their families, and also for those who are involved with voluntary organisations or statutory services for people with disabilities. I hope it will be of use to many people and, if it helps one person with disabilities find a satisfying job, all the research and writing will have been worthwhile!

When researching the book I talked to many disabled people and those who work with them. I discovered that some disabled people are able to follow or resume a career of their choice: they enjoy work, they are successful, and colleagues do not think of them as 'disabled'. However, for others, when it comes to choosing a career or finding employment, they are restricted by their disabilities, and sometimes have great difficulty in finding any type of employment.

A great variety of courses, careers, self-employment ideas and opportunities for service are explored throughout the book. The information is not confined to schemes and ideas intended exclusively for disabled people. Readers are encouraged to look at the whole field of employment and sources of help available for anyone who is searching for employment.

People with disabilities are individuals, with their own experience, gifts and skills; often they are able to work happily and responsibly alongside able-bodied people — there is no need for them to be segregated into special schemes 'for the disabled'. It is important that integration should be applied to disabled people and employment just as it is to other sections of contemporary society.

A job can give people confidence and help them to minimise a disability. Although someone may be different from a colleague because he or she wears an artificial limb, needs a wheelchair, or relies on a hearing aid or lip-reading, the person with disabilities can still have much in common with colleagues. He may enjoy the same interests, display the same professional qualities, and belong to the same association or union.

A disabled person may have added qualities of courage, determination and persistence. This book contains examples of people who have coped with handicaps, used their skill and imagination, and worked hard to achieve a full and creative way of living.

I believe that doing a job that uses one's capabilities, that is purposeful and enjoyable and brings contact with other people, can make a great difference to any person's life. It may be true that 'money isn't everything', but having a job that also brings sufficient income for basic needs, plus enough for holidays, outings, hobbies, occasional luxuries and gifts to others certainly enriches life. Creating an article of beauty, making a useful item, preparing a meal enjoyed by family and friends, or performing some service through a conversation, action, telephone call or letter can give a day more purpose. Those who can carry out such activities — and be paid for them — are fortunate indeed.

If you are looking for employment for yourself or other people I suggest you read all through this book. As you read, make a note of any suggestions you find useful. There may be some items which you could think about, adopt, or take as pointers. The book is intended to spark off ideas and help people discover new opportunities rather than presenting a blueprint. We all have some positive qualities to offer: if you are a disabled person don't doubt your own capabilities, just look at them realistically, and think how and where you could put them to good use. Addresses are given in Chapter 14.

Finding a job and keeping it can be demanding for anyone, but in the words of a young woman with multiple sclerosis, 'Most people expect you to be heroic — that is their picture of disabled people; it is really hard, but when you are trying to hold down a job you have to pretend to feel better than you do. Give an employer good value and let him see that you are a particularly reliable person.'

I am most grateful to all the people with disabilities, and the voluntary and statutory workers, who have spared the time to talk to me while I was preparing this book.

Chapter 1

Making a Choice – to Work or not to Work

When a disabled person is deciding whether to resume or take up a career, apply for training, or search for a job, there are many factors to consider.

Factors in the decision

- General health
- Strength
- Energy levels
- Mobility
- The urgency of the need to earn
- The financial benefits of working in relation to benefits received while not working
- How much a job is really wanted.

Some may feel that they would be able to work – given certain changes in their situation. For example:

- Housing near public transport
- Living in a different area
- Acquiring a car and learning to drive (mobility is discussed fully in Chapter 11)
- Being re-trained or gaining a new skill or qualification.

Perhaps aids, facilities, adaptations provided by a previous employer (with help from MSC grants) would make it easier for a person to resume the job held before illness or injury? Is it possible to be promoted or moved sideways to a different job of equal status? A person who becomes disabled should not automatically accept a downgrading. However, eventually it may be decided that downgrading is better than no job at all. Hopefully, the person will soon be able to prove that he or she is still of value to the company. After talking it over with friends and relations, and perhaps with a trade union representative, disabled people must make their own decisions about downgrading or changing jobs.

When a person is keen to do a job, or return to an old one, and the employer seems reluctant to allow this, they could consider the Job Introduction Scheme whereby a disabled person can be employed for a trial period with the MSC making a contribution towards the wage or salary paid during that time. A similar scheme, operated through MENCAP, allows a mentally handicapped person to do a job for a trial period. Details from Mencap Pathway Employment Service.

However, those who feel life is full, happy, satisfying, financially bearable, and generally less stressful because they do not work, may decide to settle for non-employment, but they should ask themselves first:

- Is my life sufficiently stimulating?
- Would it be better for me to mix with more people?
- If I do not look for a job now, will I get a job if I change my mind later on? (Some employers are wary of people who have not worked for a long time.)
- Should I work because of the special training I have received, or because of all the help I have been given by doctors, therapists, friends, family and organisations?
- If I resume my old career, or find a new one, will it show people in the Health Service, voluntary bodies, the local community, family and friends, that a disabled person can lead a normal life? Will it encourage them to invest money and effort in schemes and services that enable disabled people to become independent?

Although people may be unable to work at present, the situation could change. Can they use current free time to prepare for new and different work in the future?

Making a career change

Sudden disability may give an opportunity to make a career change, or leave work that was never really enjoyed. The decision may be forced upon people by an employer who does not wish, or will not make the effort, to keep them on. It may clearly be impossible for someone to return to the work he did previously. In either case, a step vaguely contemplated for years may now be an exciting possibility. For some people compensation or insurance money may provide the capital needed for the business they had always hoped to start.

For people who have become disabled and lost a job, the

same advice applies as to anyone who has become redundant: do not think of yourself in that light. A particular job or career may no longer be available to you, but you are not redundant as a person, you are still an individual who counts — a person who is of value to family, friends, and the community.

Martin Shail, an ex detective constable, who was blinded in a road accident, has become a furniture maker. He attended a Rehabilitation Centre and asked for a course on making rustic furniture. There was no such course available, but in the face of his determination it was decided that one should be provided. Six months later some of his superb work was put on show at the Centre, ready for sale.

Hard though it is, once people become disabled, lose a job, or meet some other misfortune, it is unproductive to keep comparing their current situation with their past. It is better to use thought, creativity and energy to do the best possible in the new situation. 'Concentrate on what you can do — not what you can't,' is good advice.

The worst thing for anyone is to allow themselves to feel dejected and rejected. For all the training schemes, career guidance, welfare workers, organisations for the disabled, in the end most people have to help themselves. It is useless to think: 'I could do . . . but no one will give me the chance.' So often in life no one does give people the chance. They have to do something — take a training course, search for a job, learn a new skill. This book is intended to give some ideas and lines that people with disabilities can follow up when considering the future.

New careers

An accident or illness may have given a person more time to think out what he or she really wants to do with the rest of life. Perhaps the illness or accident was so severe it is a bonus just to be alive.

A recently disabled person may have a chance to train for completely new work. Before making a dramatic change, consider:

- The years spent acquiring skills, experience and qualifications, and how to make the best use of these assets. Will they be wasted if a change is made?
- Whether the person is prepared to start at the bottom in a new career.

- The limitation of the person's new physical condition.

A career change is not irreversible. People may decide later that they have made a mistake. There may be no local openings or facilities for training in the chosen new field. There is need to be flexible about plans, imaginative, and open to new ideas.

Perhaps a hobby or interest can become a career? Those who enjoy playing the piano and can still play quite well could find out if any local pubs, clubs, schools want a pianist. (Suggestions for using hobbies in self-employment are contained in Chapter 8.)

Has a new career suggested itself as a result of recent experience? Is it possible to train as a social worker or therapist of some kind?

Can the person do his old job in a different way? For instance, a teacher no longer able to work in a classroom may be able to change to correspondence tutoring or private coaching.

Looking at jobs

A person who is disabled should not be too ready to give up the idea of working. Often it is a case of finding the right course or job for the present moment. This book will suggest ideas to explore and opportunities to consider.

Given the mental ability, persistence, enthusiasm, training and/or qualifications and experience, there are many spheres where a disabled person can do a job as well as an able-bodied person. Sometimes the disabled person is better. As one quite severely disabled person, Ken, a DHSS Executive Officer, told me: 'Disabled people are good workers because they have the commitment; they have to prove that they are able to do the job.'

So often the problem is being accepted for the job or training in the first place. Any unemployed person keen to find a new career needs persistence, courage and initiative.

Disabled people are not the only ones searching for new careers — there are also those who have been affected by redundancy, technological developments, or failure of an industry, service or business. A disabled person who has already had to struggle to recover from an accident or injury, or to overcome the effects of handicaps, may have developed the qualities needed for job-searching and be in a stronger position than other unemployed people. Sadly, a disabled person may have encountered rebuffs and some people's lack of confidence in him or her, or suffered from patronising attitudes. On the positive side such experiences can make a person more determined to succeed.

Alfred, who lost a leg in an air raid in World War 2, left school at 14 and became apprenticed as an instrument maker. However, he was keen to become an optician, and so he studied in the evenings after a long day's work in a factory, and passed all the exams as he went along. Then the method of qualification changed and it was announced that the last final examination for that course would be held in Liverpool. Though he found walking and travelling difficult and tiring — there was little special provision for disabled people in those days — he went to Liverpool, took the examination and passed. He is now a highly regarded optician with a well equipped practice and a host of grateful patients. Most of them would be surprised to know that his amputation and false limb still cause him great discomfort.

Alternatives to work

Depending on personality, some people may see a career or work as only one part of living. Work is not — or is no longer — one of the most important aspects of life for them. After all, there are millions of retired people living full, creative lives. 'I don't know how I ever found time to go to work,' is often a comment.

Perhaps non-employment is an opportunity to develop intellectually and spiritually, a chance to spend more time with friends and relations, a time to ponder, meditate, and relax. It may also be a time of service to other people.

Jean, who is 31, has spina bifida, and her husband David, who is 37, has brittle bones. Both are in wheelchairs. They live in a ground floor flat and do their own cleaning, shopping and cooking. Driving and caravanning are important to them, and they feel strongly that disabled people need good advice and instruction when they are learning to drive.

For at least three days each week and sometimes in the evenings they work for the local Mobility Information Service running driving assessment sessions for disabled people who want to learn to drive. They also give them advice on choosing a vehicle. In addition they tow the assessment trailer to other centres and organisations in different parts of Britain.

Retaining a job

For those who are employed there is much to be said for staying in the job until another is found. At least they do have a job — even though it may be uncongenial — and they are demonstrating an ability to work. The person who is already working often seems to be the one preferred by interviewers. As one disabled person explained: 'Once you are "in" it is easy; getting accepted in the first place is the difficulty.'

After an accident, illness or injury, it is probably best for a person to go back to his old job if he gets the chance; he could hang on until something better turns up, or until he feels fitter and more able to cope. It is worth cutting down on social life, resting more, or spending money on taxis, in order to keep a job.

If a person's employer tries to get rid of him on grounds of inability to do the job, the situation should be discussed with the employer. The disabled person could perhaps suggest ways in which to improve matters or do alternative work. It is a help if he shows that he is keen and prepared to be fair. It may be worth compromising and doing fewer hours for less salary, rather than losing the job.

Those who are threatened with dismissal that seems unfair should consult their trade union representative. They should be prepared to fight and take the case to the Advisory, Conciliation and Arbitration Service (ACAS) if necessary. It is an offence for an employer to discharge a registered disabled person, contrary to the provisions of the Quota Scheme, without reasonable cause. But note the word 'reasonable'.

Returning to work after absence

For those who have been away from work for a long time because of an accident, illness, treatment, or a deterioration in a condition, the thought of resuming work can be daunting. Yet returning to work is a big step towards recovery and normality. Preparation involves:

- Getting used to being with people in a normal situation — a family group, social club, pub, church — wherever they feel at ease.
- Asking friends into one's home; accepting invitations to visit friends or go out with them.
- Keeping up to date with news, current popular TV

programmes, record hits, and the interests of contemporaries. The extra leisure should have given time to enjoy radio, TV, papers and books. Being well-informed and able to chat naturally in a lively, interesting manner is an asset.

● Using the time to think and learn about one's job, trade or profession. Studying a professional or trade journal. Being informed about current innovations, advances and experiments in the field. It may be possible to come up with some good idea for improved efficiency and production. They could think about the problems, techniques, practices and methods in the place where they work.

● Where possible, the person should return to the habit of getting up at a regular time and dressing as if going to work. He should eat at regular times and be organised. It is wise to curtail talk about the accident, operation, or condition, to think twice before saying, 'When I was in hospital . . .' Most people do not want to be thought of as an invalid or as a patient. Emphasise the recovery if that is possible.

When back at work, the disabled person should smile, do his best — even if it is a strain — and not allow people to think, 'He is not up to it now . . .' He should become as fit as possible, observe any dietary restrictions, take the recommended exercise and rest, and accept any physiotherapy or other rehabilitation treatment offered.

Housing

Perhaps it is housing that makes it difficult for the person with disabilities to go to work. Those dependent on reliable lifts or transport services, having to negotiate stairs, steps or a steep path, should consider moving. This may involve:

● Selling a property and buying one that is more convenient
● Applying to a local council for re-housing
● Studying advertisements for council house and flat exchanges
● Advertising in a paper or on a notice board for an exchange
● Applying to a housing association or similar body.

Those who live in an institution may feel that if only they could live independently in adapted accommodation in an urban area, working would be easier. Some charities, organisations and councils do provide such housing.

Case study

In 'Making Our Way', a booklet published by the Association for Spina Bifida and Hydrocephalus (ASBAH) a number of young people describe how they have learnt to live independently.

Trevor, who is confined to a wheelchair, lived at home with his parents for 24 years. He relied on them and on friends for care, security and social life. Then he heard a consultant give a talk at a local group for disabled people. The consultant pointed out that disabled people ought not to be utterly dependent on friends and relations. This jolted Trevor.

At that time he could do little for himself, but slowly he set about learning. When an occupational therapist called to discuss fitting a hoist over Trevor's bed, she told him about some new bungalows the local council had built for disabled people. He put his name on a list and was offered a bungalow a month later, but then he had to have treatment for a bad pressure sore. After 18 weeks in hospital he moved to his bungalow and is surviving there with the support of his parents, friends and the Family Aids service who call four times a day to change his dressing and help him get up and get into bed, and look after the bungalow. So far, Trevor has not been able to find a job, but he works voluntarily one day a week in the local telephone advice service for disabled people. He also goes to a club run by disabled people for disabled people, and plays bowls in the sports centre at a spinal unit.

Although Trevor still needs the support of the Family Aids service he is gradually becoming less dependent on them — especially as their evening call comes before he wants to go to bed!

Trevor keeps himself busy; he dusts, sweeps, and enjoys going shopping in a pedestrian precinct.

It has taken much patience and restraint on the part of his parents — his mother in particular — but they understand Trevor's need to become independent. They have resisted the urge to help him constantly, and encouraged him to settle into the bungalow — because that is what he wants.

Moving to a new location

In Winchester the unemployment rate is 5.3 per cent, nearly

25 per cent of the households have at least two cars, and the number of jobs expanded by 7 per cent in the five years to 1981. In Consett, Co Durham, there is 25 per cent unemployment, only 11 per cent of households have two cars and the number of jobs fell by 33 per cent in the five years to 1981 (the *Sunday Times*, 29 September 1985).

Bearing this in mind, perhaps prospects would be better if the disabled person moved to a different part of the country, or from a rural area to a town. New towns, such as Bracknell, Milton Keynes and Basingstoke rank among the top 50 towns for prosperity.

Obviously, such a step needs careful consideration. It helps if there are friends, relatives or contacts in the new area. The quality of local social services is also worth investigating; places with a large population of elderly people may offer disabled people less help because there are already heavy demands on their services.

Those who have thought of developing any kind of craft business would probably find it worth considering moving to an area that attracts tourists with money to spend.

Anyone who has reduced mobility, greater susceptibility to cold, or more vulnerability in snowy and icy weather, as a result of illness or injury, may want to think about finding somewhere with a milder climate.

One of the problems when moving to a more prosperous area is that house prices are likely to be higher. On the other hand, this may be the stage of life when a smaller house would be easier for you, or it could be a chance to move to a bungalow. Ask a DRO or Jobcentre about the possibilities of help with the cost of finding and moving to a job in a different part of the country.

Personal services

It may be a good idea to review any personal care the individual receives. If, for instance, he relies on a district nurse or voluntary agency workers who visit at unpredictable times and keep him waiting at home, it may be easier to pay someone to come privately at the disabled person's convenience. Though this will make a dent in earnings, it could be worth considering if it would liberate someone enough to take a job.

Life after an accident or injury

People who have been disabled after an accident or injury

may be waiting for the results of a claim or court case concerning compensation. Information about benefits, claims and appeals is contained in Leaflet NI 6/April 1983, issued by the DHSS. They may also need advice from a trade union, an ex-service organisation or a solicitor; a Citizens' Advice Bureau should be able to give information about legal aid.

They should try not to spend all their time and energy worrying about the case, the compensation they might receive, and who was to blame for the accident. They need to get on with living and make the most of all their remaining abilities. The people who can do this seem to be the happiest and most fulfilled. I once knew a man who was consumed with bitterness towards the motorist who had killed his wife and injured him. Even people with the deepest sympathy found it hard to befriend him.

Be positive. Perhaps there is something that can be done to prevent someone else having a similar accident. It may have been caused by a hazardous crossing, a faulty tool, an unguarded machine, or someone's own carelessness. See that other people are made aware of the danger.

Disclosing the disability

When disabled people apply for a job, they will have to decide whether or not to mention the fact that they are disabled. Before making this decision, the following points should be considered:

- If an application form asks the candidate to describe his state of health and he gives false information, this may go against him if the disability becomes apparent at the interview. If he manages to conceal his disability, but it subsequently comes to light, he could be dismissed. In letters of application, describe qualifications and experience and hope to gain an interview on the strength of these. Those selected for interview could then explain their disability and say how little it would interfere with their work.

- Some employers positively welcome applications from disabled people as it helps them to fulfil their quota. In this case a disability may be an advantage.

Only the individual can decide which course of action to choose. Trial and error may show the best strategy to adopt. In any case it will help if the disability is explained clearly and simply, with examples of people with similar disabilities who are working successfully.

Obtaining advice

A DRO should be able to advise about career change, training and employment prospects. He or she should be able to tell the disabled person about all the statutory help to which he is entitled and about schemes for helping people to set up in business. But disabled people also need to discuss their position with someone who knows them as people, who appreciates their gifts and abilities. It helps to talk to people in different professions and jobs. It is important to listen to the radio; read widely; be ever on the look-out for information and ideas about possible jobs. Such things as a talk on Woman's Hour, an article in a local paper, or a newspaper's regular features on careers, could all give pointers.

Organisations and local authority services for disabled people may also be able to offer advice (see Chapters 2 and 4).

Those people considering whether or not to return to work, and those seeking a new career, should study the government leaflets intended to help people in such circumstances. There is 'Executive Job-hunting for People with Health Problems or Disability' from Professional and Executive Recruitment (PER); 'Unemployed' FB 9/Jan 85 (or later editions) from any DHSS office; *Occupations*, an authoritative MSC guide to careers and job change.

An abundance of literature is produced by the DHSS, MSC, local authorities and organisations, much of which is mentioned in this book.

Chapter 2

Employment for People with Disabilities

Introduction

In this chapter some of the provisions, services and aids for people with disabilities are described, and sources of further information are given.

The benefits of registering as a disabled person are discussed and the 'Fit for Work' campaign, aimed at making employers aware that disabled people can become 'good, steady and productive workers', is mentioned.

Attention is drawn to the Code of Good Practice on the Employment of Disabled People, and the British Standards Institution's recommendations on access for disabled people are noted. Those who are disabled are urged to check environmental safety points in any place where they work, and there are suggestions on how to set about negotiating improvements.

DHSS benefits for disabled people are listed and the expense of living as a disabled person is briefly discussed.

If someone is or has become disabled the Manpower Services Commission is keen to help. There is a range of services and provisions for disabled people, and it is well worth finding out about all of them.

Disablement Resettlement Officers (DROs)

These specially trained officers are the first people a disabled person (over 18) should contact. They are based at larger Jobcentres and visit smaller centres on certain days each week. If you have never consulted a DRO, or have not seen one for some time, look in the telephone directory for the address of your nearest large Jobcentre and phone to make an appointment. A home visit can be arranged if necessary.

DROs will be able to point to the relevant literature, describe all the statutory services the disabled person would be eligible to use, and give an idea of the local employment prospects.

The service is, of course, free; there is nothing to lose by contacting DROs, and even if they do not come up with a concrete solution to the employment problem, those who contact them are bound to learn something from them.

Job Introduction Scheme

Through this scheme the MSC pays a firm a weekly fee for six weeks while a disabled person works with that firm on trial.

Aids and adaptations at the workplace

Free, indefinite loans of aids and tools needed to help a disabled person obtain or keep employment are available. In 1984, 1640 special aids to employment were loaned to disabled workers, and 145 employers received grants for adapting premises and equipment.

Typewriters can be adapted, special chairs provided, ramps can be installed for wheelchairs, and flashing lights added to fire alarms. Sometimes equipment does not need to be modified, it simply needs rearranging so that, for example, a person in a wheelchair can work at a desk more easily.

Disablement Advisory Service (DAS)

Employers can obtain practical advice and financial help from the DAS, which has been set up by the MSC especially to help employers make full use of the skills and abilities of disabled people.

Fares to work

Severely disabled people who are unable to use public transport to travel to work can receive MSC help for up to 75 per cent of the cost of taxi travel to work. A maximum weekly amount is fixed for each person.

Personal reader service

The MSC can provide assistance with the cost of a part-time personal reader to assist a visually handicapped person with his or her work. (To find out more about this scheme consult the Royal National Institute for the Blind.)

Sheltered Industrial Groups

Small groups of severely disabled people are sometimes employed on business premises. The firm provides the necessary equipment and pays a sponsor — usually a local authority, voluntary organisation or Remploy — for the work carried out by each person. The sponsor and the MSC pay the people in the group. Individuals can be employed in a similar way through the Sheltered Placement Scheme, described in Chapter 6.

Employment rehabilitation centres

The MSC has 27 rehabilitation centres where a variety of courses are offered and disabled people can be assessed and advised about future employment. (For more details see Chapter 6.)

The Disabled Persons Register

To qualify for this register a person must be 'substantially handicapped by injury, disease or congenital deformity' and have difficulty in obtaining employment suited to his or her age, qualifications and experience. The disability must be likely to continue for at least 12 months, and the person must want to obtain employment.

Should you register?

Registration is entirely voluntary. Some disabled people decide against it because they are afraid they will be labelled 'disabled', and others do not need to register because they manage perfectly well without it. Those who do register can ask (in writing) for their names to be removed at any time.

Advantages of registration

Every employer with 20 or more employees has a duty under the Disabled Persons (Employment) Act to employ a quota — at present 3 per cent — of disabled persons. Unfortunately, it is not obligatory to fulfil this quota, and only about one-third of employers do so. Nonetheless, the provision is there and it is intended to help those on the register to find work.

Vacancies for car park attendants and passenger electric lift attendants are reserved for registered disabled people. You may think this is of doubtful value as it only reinforces the idea that such work is what disabled people want to do, when so many disabled people are capable of doing more demanding work. Nevertheless, this facility is provided and may benefit the right person.

Employment in sheltered workshops also is often reserved for registered disabled people.

Disabled people who have been unemployed for eight of the previous 15 months, and disabled people aged 18 to 24 years who have been unemployed for four out of the previous nine months, receive priority when applying for Community Programme jobs. Disabled young people also receive priority on Youth Training Schemes.

It is an offence for an employer to dismiss a registered disabled worker without reasonable cause if the employer is below quota or will fall below quota by doing so.

When they produce their annual reports, companies with more than 250 employees are required to include a statement on their policies concerning the employment of disabled people. This reminds them of their responsibilities towards disabled people and may mean that more opportunities are offered to those who are on the list.

Some of the special assistance mentioned earlier in the chapter is offered to registered disabled people only.

Applying for registration

The Jobcentre, or careers office for school-leavers, will explain how to apply; alternatively, a Specialist Careers Adviser or DRO will guide the person concerned. It is not necessary to be unemployed to register; any disabled people can apply. They will be asked to produce evidence, such as a disability pension book or a form completed by their doctor. If there is still doubt about eligibility, they will probably be asked to attend a panel drawn from a local Committee for the Employment of Disabled People. A trade union representative or someone from an organisation concerned with disabled people will be allowed to accompany those who attend.

Those accepted for registration will be given a certificate lasting from one to ten years. The expiry date will be shown on the certificate, and renewal should be applied for about two months beforehand. The names will be added to the local Jobcentre's list of registered disabled people, and the Jobcentre should let them know when suitable vacancies arise.

Further information
The MSC publishes a leaflet, 'The Disabled Persons Register'. Copies should be available at Jobcentres. It also produces a number of leaflets for employers. Anyone with a specific disability would find it worth obtaining the relevant leaflet — for example, 'Employing Someone with Epilepsy' — studying it and taking it along to interviews. The prospective employer may not have seen it, and also it is useful to find out what sort of information and advice employers are given. A full list of these leaflets appears in 'Employing Disabled People — Sources of Help' (EPL 147).

MSC leaflet DPL2, 'The Disabled Persons (Employment) Acts 1944 and 1958', is also informative.

Ex-service men and women

When selecting disabled people for training courses and employment the MSC must give preference to ex-service men and women if there are several candidates who are equally suitable.

'Fit for Work' campaign

With the support of the government, the Confederation of British Industries and the Trades Union Congress (TUC), an MSC Fit for Work campaign was launched in 1979. It aims to make employers more aware that disabled people can become 'good, steady and productive workers'. In 1984 it launched a 'Code of Good Practice on the Employment of Disabled People' to give guidance to senior management on the training and re-training of disabled people.

To encourage employers to follow this code there is an award scheme, and winners may display the 'Fit for Work' symbol on their stationery and promotional material. In 1985 the award was won by 101 companies.

Examples of winners' achievements
Tuppen and Jones Ltd, Deeside, make highly fragile spun-glass ornaments. Out of a workforce of 11 there are five disabled people. One is a polio sufferer, two have lower limb disabilities, one has spina bifida and another is epileptic.

At British Aerospace, Blackburn, a young man who lost a leg in a motorbike accident is back at the factory where he used to be a fitter. He is now doing a job specially restructured for him.

This factory employs about 3050 people — 10 per cent of them disabled.

Ros Reed has been disabled through polio since she was six months old. Now aged 39, she has been employed by Cadbury's at Somerdale, Keynsham, Bristol, for 20 years and is secretary to the technical manager.

In the Department of Fluid Engineering and Instrumentation at Cranfield Institute of Technology, four of the graduate employees are severely physically handicapped. With help and equipment from the MSC, the Nuffield Foundation and the Gatby Charitable Foundation, a blind graduate and a profoundly deaf graduate are happily working there in full-time research. Two others, including a tetraplegic engineer, are working part-time from home.

Code of Good Practice on the Employment of Disabled People

The Code was launched in November 1984. It is addressed to directors, senior management, personnel and other managers, and it is for the use of large and small employers in both the private and public sectors.

The code is concerned with all disabled workers and not only those who are registered. It makes suggestions for deciding on a policy towards the employment of disabled people; sets out the law relating to the employment of disabled people; examines some concerns of employers about employing disabled people; and describes some of the help available (eg a special drawing board provided through the MSC for a young marine engineer, confined to a wheelchair after an accident, but engaged to operate a typesetting machine and to design art work). It also gives advice on recruiting, selecting and interviewing. There are recommendations such as 'Allow a deaf or speech-impaired person to bring an interpreter . . .' and 'ensure that a place of interview is accessible to any candidate with a mobility handicap, or that assistance is available to help them on arrival.'

The whole document is practical and positive: 'Managers may overlook or underestimate the potential of disabled workers. This code enables companies to examine their objectives towards disabled workers so that they can benefit fully from proven skills, abilities and commitment.' If you meet an employer who has not seen this document, tell him or her it is available through the MSC Disablement Advisory Service.

Further information

All these and other schemes are described in detail in leaflets produced, and constantly being updated, by the MSC. Look for them in Jobcentres, ask a DRO for copies, or write to the MSC. It is worth studying the leaflets carefully and being familiar with all the provisions — do not rely on an employer knowing all about what is available. You could also obtain the literature published for employers. 'Employing Disabled People — Sources of Help' is a good, comprehensive guide. You might be glad to have a copy with you when being interviewed by an employer who wants to help you. The 'TUC Guide on the Employment of Disabled People' also contains a great deal of useful information.

Access

Legislation on access for disabled people is contained in a number of Acts and regulations, but it has been difficult to enforce these in older buildings. They are far more likely to be respected in new buildings. So when searching for training or work, disabled people are advised to look out for new colleges, shops, factories and office blocks. These are British Standards Institution recommendations that feature in new and proposed regulations:

- Pedestrian routes kept free of obstructions
- Pathways wide enough for wheelchairs
- Pathway surfaces slip resistant
- Shallow ramps at changes in level
- Handrails by steps and stairs
- Doors easy to open and wide enough for a wheelchair
- In a multi-storey building at least one lift with controls which can be worked by a person in a wheelchair
- Slip-resistant floor surfaces
- Signposts legible and well illuminated
- Names and numerals at a low level on doors
- Audible signals such as alarms linked to visual signals such as flashing lights
- Switches and ventilation controls within easy reach of people in wheelchairs
- A well-known and practised route for helping disabled people leave the building in an emergency
- No-smoking areas for people with heart or chest complaints

- An induction loop system to help the hard of hearing at meetings*
- At least one toilet suitable for people with disabilities.

You could look around the place where you are working, or hope to work, and see how far these recommendations are observed. You need to think of your own safety. You know what the particular potential dangers and difficulties are for you personally — slippery steps, a carelessly placed rubbish bin where you expect the path to be clear, or being marooned on the top floor when the only lift is out of action.

Improvements may need to be negotiated through a trade union representative, a welfare officer, or by your own efforts. Ultimately, however, you are the person who will have to decide whether or not you can work in a particular building in comfort and safety.

You may also need to look at parking facilities. Perhaps the company or organisation would be willing to create a parking bay that would be convenient for you.

Working environment

'Work fit for people and people fit for work' is the World Health Organisation's slogan for occupational health. Professor Charles Rossiter and his small staff at the University of London Department of Occupational Health concentrate on two aspects of occupational health — the working environment and matching people to suitable jobs.

Research is continuing all the time, and the effects of dust, heat, fumes, strong or inadequate lighting, noise, chemicals, air conditioning and ventilation are being considered and remedies sought where there is a problem. Disabled people should look at the whole work environment — they may feel they could not tolerate the conditions. On the other hand, simple remedies,

* An induction loop system enables hard of hearing people to hear only the sound coming directly from the microphone or public address system; additional, unwanted noises are cut out. To benefit from the system the hard of hearing person needs to wear the correct type of hearing aid behind the ear and with a suitable setting. These systems are installed in churches, halls, theatres, cinemas and other entertainment centres. Local organisations for disabled or deaf and hard of hearing people should have lists of places where the system has been installed. In London the Greater London Association for Disabled People (GLAD) can give information about the system and where it has been installed. For advice on using the system, contact the Royal National Institute for the Deaf.

such as cling film wrapped around a piece of equipment producing dust, may improve things.

Disabled people should be able to discuss any problems with a personnel or welfare officer, or with a trade union representative. Tact will be needed. They should not expect employers to make too many concessions and changes just for them, but it should be made clear that they can do the job without inconveniencing other people or being a burden on the employer.

Equal opportunities

The Equal Pay Act aims to remove discrimination between men and women in pay and terms of employment. If a woman feels that there is discrimination against her — compared with a similarly disabled man — she can make a claim before an Industrial Tribunal in the same way as any non-disabled woman, but it is likely to be very difficult to prove. For advice consult the Equal Opportunities Commission. A free leaflet, 'Equal Pay for Work of Equal Value', is available from the Commission and in some libraries and Citizens' Advice Bureaux. Sisters Against Disability is specially concerned about women with disabilities.

Organisations

There are now a great many national organisations concerned with the welfare of disabled people. Some of these have staff and departments that specialise in giving advice on training and employment. Whatever your particular disability, it is worth approaching the relevant organisation, or a comprehensive body such as the Royal Association for Disability and Rehabilitation (RADAR), the Scottish Council on Disability, Wales Council for the Disabled or Northern Ireland Council for the Handicapped, to see what they have to offer.

Provision by organisations such as the Spastics Society is described in Chapter 5 and elsewhere in this book. Useful addresses are listed in Appendix 2.

The Royal National Institute for the Blind and the Royal National Institute for the Deaf have particularly good services to offer eligible people. If sight and/or hearing difficulties are handicapping someone in obtaining employment, he should not hesitate to contact these organisations.

The Association for Spina Bifida and Hydrocephalus has a booklet, 'Making Our Way', which contains some heartening stories of people who are courageously coping with severe problems. It is a book for everyone to read and appreciate — disabled people, parents of disabled children and the non-disabled.

The book is realistic and does not pretend that all the provision is ideal. One person says: 'Schooling locally proved a dismal failure'. He eventually decided he would like to be an architectural draughtsman: 'I started out wanting to be an architect, but realised this wasn't practical because of having to go out on site so often. The draughtsman job was alright until we went out on site into fields knee high in grass. I realised it would be no good.' He is now working as an apprentice typesetter.

Sian, who is 22, has to cope with the problems of being in a wheelchair, and she is forced to rely on other people if she wants to go out anywhere because her home is on a steep hillside in a Welsh mining valley. The ramp from her house is so steep she cannot even go into the back garden alone because her chair could so easily tip over. Sian went to a residential further education college for disabled students, but unfortunately she didn't achieve much educationally. 'We had to do all our own washing and ironing, and quite honestly I found it too much with having to study as well . . .' For her, the most helpful thing has been the opening of a local day centre for younger disabled people. Here she has met other people of her own age, and she has enjoyed getting to know the mothers and babies who attend a group that also meets there.

When I was doing research before writing this book I went to public libraries and worked through folders and boxes containing information on all the organisations and services for disabled people in three London boroughs. What struck me was how few mentioned 'employment' in their aims and objectives. Leisure activities, outings, transport, social get-togethers appeared over and over again. Important and beneficial though these activities may be, helping people aged 16 to 60 to find a satisfying job that brings independence and a normal adult life style is surely the highest priority. Try to find out what your borough and local organisations offer as far as employment and rehabilitation are concerned. If there is an urgent need for more provision perhaps you could discuss this with a local councillor.

DHSS benefits for disabled people

The pattern of benefits for disabled people is largely based on the cause of disability rather than its severity, and can be a factor when deciding whether or not to seek employment. The main benefits for disabled people are:

- Invalidity pension
- Invalidity allowance
- Industrial injury benefit
- Industrial disablement pension
- War pension
- Attendance allowance
- Invalid care allowance
- Mobility allowance
- Non-contributory invalidity pension
- Supplementary benefit
- Numerous additional payments such as those for heating and diet.

They are all clearly set out in 'Help for Handicapped People', available from the DHSS Leaflets Unit. All disabled people (or their carers) should study this leaflet for up-to-date information and advice on how to claim the various allowances.

The whole system of benefits is complex and changes frequently. It is worthwhile finding out for yourself about the different allowances and extra payments for which you may be eligible. Social workers, the Citizens' Advice Bureau (CAB), and local government advice services should be able to help you, as well as organisations such as the Royal Association for Disability and Rehabilitation (RADAR). But do not rely entirely on these for up-to-date, accurate information. If you are unable to visit your local DHSS office, it is wise to make an appointment and ask for a home visit. Advice can also be obtained by dialling 100 and asking for Freefone DHSS.

In a report published on 23 June 1986 the National Consumer Council called for a larger network of centres to give advice on money, housing and other matters of concern — including employment. Mobile advice centres were suggested for rural areas which are poorly served.

The report says that in spite of the work of agencies such as CAB the services are inadequate. People are left to cope 'with the endless strain of unemployment and job-hunting while struggling to make ends meet on a low income . . .' said Mr Michael Montague, the Council chairman.

Cost of living

Disabled people often face higher costs than the non-disabled. Housing, warmth and food may entail extra expense, and difficulties in using transport may mean that disabled people cannot shop around and compare prices, or they have to use a car and spend money on petrol for short errands that an able-bodied person could accomplish on foot. For some disabled people there is extra wear on clothing because callipers, artificial limbs, and straps cause damage and shorten the life of clothing. Some disabled people need to buy special equipment and incontinence aids.

In a survey published by the General and Municipal Workers Union, it is reported that disabled people 'suffer lower levels of income and less access to resources than their non-disabled counterparts'. A DHSS survey of 1975 showed that 68 per cent of severely incapacitated people were living with incomes below or on the margins of the state's standard of poverty.

Incomes

The concept of a comprehensive disability allowance, based on the degree of handicap, not the cause, is gaining acceptance, largely through the campaigning of the Disability Alliance, but implementation is hardly in sight. In the meantime many disabled people are living on low incomes. Even those with jobs in sheltered workshops and with organisations are often poorly paid and little better off than those who depend on benefits.

To earn an income comparable with those enjoyed by able-bodied contemporaries with similar abilities, it is necessary to find a career or self-employment opportunity. It is worth training, searching hard, and being imaginative enough to find an occupation that is rewarding and satisfying — but it is not easy. It takes courage and perseverance. But many disabled people do succeed.

Megan Au Boisson, whose letter to a newspaper (Guardian Women) resulted in the formation of the Disablement Incomes Group (DIG), fought for the right of disabled people to a pension irrespective of the reason for disability.

People who are disabled suffer the same disadvantages

whether their condition is caused by arthritis, polio, multiple sclerosis, a road accident, industrial injury or in the course of service in the police, fire brigade or armed forces, but the level of compensation and/or pension varies greatly. DIG is still fighting for equality of rights for disabled people and for recognition of the fact that living costs are greater for them.

Chapter 3

The Disabled School-Leaver

There is a need for parents, teachers, social workers, careers officers and young people themselves to think positively about their abilities. The importance of being persistent in the job-search cannot be over-emphasised. Ways in which parents can familiarise disabled youngsters with the world of work are suggested in this chapter, and there are pointers towards sources of help, advice and further information.

As more than a quarter of all 16 to 18 year olds are out of work, according to the National Youth Bureau, and more than a quarter of 18 to 19 year olds, according to the MSC, it would be natural to think that disabled people in that age group could have great problems finding work. However, for disabled youngsters, as for any young person who is unemployed, there are opportunities for training or joining in community programmes and voluntary schemes — as well as help with job-searching and advice for those who want to start their own business. In many of the MSC schemes for young people, those who are disabled receive priority.

Notes for parents

It really is worthwhile for the school-leaver and his or her parents and friends to search around for possible openings. They should consider:

- Whether the young person has had all the training/education from which he or she could benefit
- What the young person wants to do with his or her life; his or her hopes, ambitions and plans
- The person's physical and mental capabilities, and any special gifts or interests
- How far the person is, or could become, independent
- Whether the person wishes to live at home, in sheltered accommodation, or alone.

It is important that young people think through their situation, discuss plans, and take steps to organise their own future. They do not want decisions made for them, but they do need to find out or be informed what is available.

The EEC Document, *Disabled People and Their Employment* (1985), stresses: 'Past training schemes are no longer relevant in a certain number of cases. New technologies are expected to change the qualifications required in the workplace.' It then points out certain elements that should be included in any vocational training programme for young disabled people. These include adjustment to technological change, improved mobility, basic skills needed for participation in training programmes, and retraining for those threatened by the introduction of micro-electronics.

Training given to young disabled people should be geared to contemporary industrial and office methods, or it should give them a skill they could use in a business of their own.

Parents, teachers, social workers and careers officers should encourage young disabled people to think positively about their abilities. It is important to look at the whole range of career possibilities and training courses, not just at those intended for disabled people. Try to make sure they study plenty of career guides and that they meet non-disabled contemporaries and hear about the kinds of career they are planning. Encourage them to obtain prospectuses from local further education colleges, specialist colleges, polytechnics and universities.

Among the success stories is a 17-year-old boy, left deaf and deformed by polio at the age of 18 months, who the disablement resettlement officer considered unemployable. He was kept on a course for three years. After the first year he travelled to college by bus, and gradually his working day was extended to seven hours. After six months' work experience with a firm making electric bulbs for headlamps, he was taken on permanently for packaging and light warehouse work.

Then there was the grammar-school boy who wanted to become a professional footballer or work in the family fish and chip shop, but both were ruled out by a rare form of thrombosis in the feet and legs. At the college he took O and A levels by the age of 20 and became president of the students' union. Now he is at Ilkley College, training to teach handicapped children, and is president of the union again.

Courses and training that a young disabled person could consider are described in Chapter 5.

Searching for employment

A young disabled person who wants a job must use his or her initiative, study advertisements, be alert to local developments, and talk to people about the kind of work being sought. A great many vacancies are never notified to Jobcentres; they are filled by people who happen to hear that someone is leaving, that a firm is expanding, or that a person is needed for a particular job.

It can be worthwhile approaching local employers and telling them what you have to offer — 'the speculative approach' as the MSC calls it.

Plenty of contacts certainly help, so mix with other people, able-bodied and disabled, and ask them how they found their jobs, and what they advise you to do. Most people love giving advice, but you don't have to accept it all.

Professional advice services

The MSC is keen to help young disabled people to find training or work. Their message to employers is: 'Don't label them: think of their potential.' To young people it stresses: 'You need an opportunity to show what you are capable of doing.'

Go to your Jobcentre and ask about all the schemes from which you could benefit; make an appointment for an interview with a DRO. Look again at the schemes and provisions outlined in Chapter 2, and ask the Jobcentre for leaflets explaining these in detail.

The MSC has a very helpful booklet, 'Working It Out, an aid to deciding about jobs'. It has pages of questions to ask yourself about your skills, personal qualities, and what you want from a job. Completing the questions could help you think out what type of job would suit you, what you have to offer an employer, and how you are going to tackle the serious business of finding the right job or career. Copies can be obtained from the MSC Careers and Occupational Information Centre, or some Jobcentres.

The school or college you attend may have a careers teacher, so make sure you have an interview with him or her before you leave.

Some organisations, such as the Spastics Society, have a Careers Advisory Service. The Spastics Society's service is designed to meet individual needs; it offers advice by telephone, puts people in touch with other sources of help, and sometimes arranges assessment courses that help to establish a young person's abilities and potential. If you suffer from cerebral palsy you are strongly advised to get in touch with this service as it specialises in helping young people approaching school-leaving age.

The Royal National Institute for the Blind, the Royal National Institute for the Deaf and MENCAP will advise those who need their specialist services. Parents of mentally handicapped young people would find 'An Ordinary Working Life, vocational services for people with mental handicap', published by King's Fund Centre, a useful guide. It emphasises the importance of choice: 'One of the fundamental principles guiding our thinking is that people should be enabled and encouraged to determine, as far as possible, the kind of work they wish to do and with whom they wish to work.'

The study paper also suggests ways in which a parent can prepare a child and orientate him or her to the world of work. Making scrap books about work, listening to stories which include information about work, visiting places of work, talking about what the child may want to do when he or she grows up, and doing part-time jobs with a brother or sister, are among the suggestions.

It adds that parents need to learn about the vocational services that support young people with handicaps, and that, after thinking about these issues, parents can begin to create pressure to 'open up more work opportunities for handicapped sons and daughters'.

The study paper is likely to be available in resource centres for disabled people and social workers.

Directory of Opportunities for School-Leavers with Disabilities

There has long been need for a comprehensive guide to all the courses, vocational training, workshops, hostels and residential units for young disabled people. Now, Queen Elizabeth's Foundation for the Disabled has produced such a guide. Provision of different types is listed alphabetically under counties in England, Scotland, Northern Ireland, and Wales, with the name of the sponsor, a note of how many people each scheme accommodates, and the subjects or facilities offered. Thus you can discover that Portadown has a workshop with picture framing, woodwork and upholstery courses, while in Dunstable,

Bedfordshire County Council operates three-year apprentice-ships in wood products, and West Sussex has a printing and craftwork hobbies centre at Lancing.

This guide would be especially useful for social workers, career advisers and organisations. Most disabled youngsters and their parents want to know about local facilities rather than those in all parts of the country, but the guide is welcome as it will help advisers to be well informed.

MSC Youth Training Scheme

In the 12 months to July 1985 about 60 per cent of 16 to 17 year old school-leavers entered the Youth Training Scheme. The advantage of the scheme is that it is open to all young people, not just to those who are disabled, though there are wider age limits for disabled young people.

The Youth Training Scheme has been criticised on the grounds that only 60 per cent of those who participate find permanent jobs or go on to further education and training. But there are two ways of looking at such statistics: two out of every three young people who have completed a YTS *have* found a job or further training; therefore the scheme is still well worth exploring if you have just left school. A careers officer or Jobcentre will advise you, but look around for yourself too.

The YTS operates in all kinds of industries and settings, and the MSC is constantly looking at ways in which it can be expanded and improved. The YTS has been called 'a training revolution'. Lord Young, Secretary of State for Employment, said recently: 'Only three years ago, young people had nothing to prepare them for work, other than a decaying, and often irrelevant apprenticeship system. Now the system has been transformed, giving a million young people a sound foundation for their working lives.' Let us hope that disabled young people will be well represented in the next million.

A survey of those who have participated in the scheme is being carried out by the MSC in preparation for introducing a new two-year scheme.

Local council training programmes

Lambeth has training programmes, sponsored by the Borough Council, with catering and clerical programmes. Any unemployed person between the ages of 16 and 17, and disabled young people under 21, are invited to join the one-year scheme. A weekly allowance of £25 is paid to all trainees, and there is help with travelling costs. But to the organisers' disappointment, no disabled young people have applied to join the scheme. The council is planning to advertise the scheme more widely from February 1986. Non-disabled young people who have participated in the scheme have found jobs in catering at London hotels or clerical work in the Council offices.

The lesson to be learnt from this story is to ask all kinds of bodies — local authorities, organisations, and social services — what is available, and to search around for opportunities for yourself or your child. Listen to local radio, read local papers, study the notices and leaflets in libraries, and talk to as many people as possible. Remember that new schemes are always being started; the situation is not static. Go back to organisations and ask them again what is available or planned. By your persistence you may show them that there is a need for a scheme and that you personally really want to work or train.

Threshold Scheme

New technology and the training and jobs it offers will be discussed in Chapter 9, but as the Threshold Scheme is especially designed for people aged 17 to 19, it is worth mentioning it here. The scheme provides a way into computing which offers many careers disabled people could enjoy. Those who have the aptitude and can pass the challenging selection tests are accepted for a 42-week course, throughout which they receive a weekly allowance. The course leads to a Business and Technician Education Council National Certificate in Computer Studies. At the end of the course most trainees obtain jobs as operators or programmers. For details apply to the National Computing Centre.

Community Programmes

These Programmes provide temporary employment, usually for one year or less. Those eligible include disabled people aged 18 to 24 who have been unemployed for four out of the previous nine months.

Some of the jobs offered through the scheme are advertised

in the MSC newspaper, *Executive Post*, but I have rarely seen any suitable for school-leavers. Most of the jobs seem to call for qualifications, managerial experience or technical training that a young person is unlikely to have acquired. However, it would be worth looking for suitable Community Programme vacancies advertised in Jobcentres and local papers.

The effects of unemployment

Young people should start looking for a job or career as soon as they have left school or college — or well before if possible. Once they get into the habit of not working or studying it will be harder to start work. Being young, unemployed and stuck in the house all day can easily cause problems. They become bored, lose status, lack money and, because they are not independent, find that they are treated like children. No disabled person wants to be over-protected or patronised. They need to show that they are individuals with capabilities and interests of their own.

Other members of the family can suffer if they are all at home together all day; tensions, even rows, are likely to develop. They can become angry, depressed, frustrated, and resentful. These feelings are a natural reaction to unemployment and the best remedy is to improve the situation.

Day and occupation centres can be boring for young people — especially if most of the other people there are elderly. Local authorities are now making greater efforts to establish such centres especially for young people. These centres may be livelier and more useful, but it is far better to mix with non-disabled people. That is the great advantage of an ordinary job in ordinary surroundings, rather than being in a place with a disproportionate number of disabled people.

If they cannot find a job, it is best to undertake some activity, sport, craft, hobby, service to other people, or join a social group that they will enjoy, and which will involve contact with non-disabled people. There are some suggestions in Chapter 12.

Young people who cannot find work and are allowed supplementary benefit will also be entitled to other benefits, such as free NHS prescriptions and dental treatment, so it is worth finding out about all the benefits available and how they can be claimed. Leaflet FB 9/Jan 85, 'Unemployment' (or later versions) obtainable from the DHSS and advice centres gives general guidance. The Social Security Office (listed under

Health and Social Security in the telephone book) will give advice.

It is most important to apply for benefit as soon as one leaves school or becomes unemployed. School-leavers can claim benefit from the first Monday in January, the first Monday after Easter, or the first Monday in September. Claims cannot usually be back-dated.

Young people's views

It is clear that most young people want to work. The Royal Association for Disability and Rehabilitation (RADAR) arranged a conference for 26 disabled people between the ages of 16 and 30 in 1984. They gave their views frankly, saying, 'There is no real alternative to work.'

Though the conference tried to look at 'significant living without work', the majority of the young people said that obtaining a job was their principal aim. The only kinds of leisure provision they wanted as an alternative to work were:

- Groups set up for or by disabled people where they could join together to fight for their needs
- Drop-in centres which they could visit when they wished.

Whether or not they obtained a job, all wanted to be as independent as possible in terms of mobility and of being allowed to take decisions for themselves.

To mark International Youth Year in 1985, RADAR tried to find out what young people themselves thought of society's attitude towards disability. Here are some comments: 'When dignitaries go visiting schools, they are always shown around the best parts and when they ask some poor kid whether he or she enjoys school or not, the answer they expect is "yes". But they never ask questions like, "Would you like to go to a mainstream school?" or, "How do you get treated by other people?" '

'Luckily I have a Dad and four brothers who treat me as normal, so I have got over that feeling of being different.'

'Being disabled has its advantages and disadvantages. The advantages are being able to park your car in most places, and getting into some public places at reduced rates or even free. Also I have done a lot more in sport than most able-bodied kids of my age. Not many able-bodied people have represented their county at athletics meetings where they compete with people from all over the country.'

'Most of us don't want mollycoddling all our lives. Most

disabled kids want as normal a life as possible, and to be treated as normally as possible.'

Finding a job

Schemes, sources of help, and ideas on looking out for jobs are mentioned throughout the book. Do use Jobcentres. Look in the telephone book to locate them. It is not essential to go to the nearest; ones further from home may provide easier parking, a greater choice of jobs, or they may seem to have more helpful staff.

Avoid visiting Jobcentres at the busiest time, such as Monday mornings. In slacker periods, you will be able to look at all the boards more easily, and staff will have more time to help you.

A Jobcentre like Brixton has about 20 vacancies coming direct to the branch each day, and well over 200 from other branches; the new vacancies board is completely changed almost twice every day. Most Jobcentres have one or two staff who take a special interest in disabled people.

A helpful information pack, 'Jobhunting', is available free at most Jobcentres. It gives advice on approaching employers, completing application forms and being interviewed. Large Jobcentres have libraries holding copies of all MSC publications.

When you go for a job interview, take with you a neatly typed piece of paper setting out the subjects you have studied, the qualifications you have gained, and your skills and interests.

Work-Out project

This project started as Jobmate with Capital Radio in London and links young unemployed people with volunteers who will advise them on training, education and job searching, and help them to work out their problems. Information and a Work-Out survival pack are available free from 8 Strutton Ground, London SW1P 2HP; phone 01-222 0222. Other cities may have similar schemes; phone your local radio station and ask about them.

Careers offices

School-leavers will probably be in touch with their local careers office. If not, those under 18 should contact them right away. They will do all they can to advise on jobs and careers. In any case, it is essential to register with them to obtain supplementary benefits and National Insurance credits.

Keeping a job

Once a suitable job is obtained, the obvious plan is to keep it. More people lose jobs through inability to get on with colleagues than through lack of skills and ability, so it is important to do one's best to get on well with the people at work and be cooperative, punctual and cheerful. Do one's share of the work and build a reputation for reliability. Try not to get drawn into gossip. Be loyal to one's company or employer. A disabled person in ordinary employment or a work scheme has a responsibility towards others who are disabled. If taking one on is a success, the employer will be more likely to recruit other disabled workers. News of disabled people's achievements soon spreads. The number of individuals who have been keen to tell me about disabled people they know, and how well these people are coping with jobs, is surprising.

There is the University of London graduate, with only one hand, who works in a publisher's office, and 19-year-old Ann who is a receptionist and typist with a finance company in Heckmondwyke. She has spina bifida and walks with sticks, and it took her some time to find a suitable job though she left school with five CSEs and then took a secretarial course. 'At some interviews I was unsuccessful because of the problem of access to the offices. There were often too many stairs, or they were too steep, or the job would have entailed carrying heavy files which I couldn't have coped with.'

As Andrew Duncan pointed out in the *Sunday Telegraph* magazine: 'It's not often that a small middle-aged man with a limp becomes a romantic film hero.' But that is what one of the world's 'highest paid sex symbols', Dudley Moore, has achieved. He was born with a club foot and the left leg one inch shorter than the right, and he stands at five foot two.'

Persevere

When one applies for jobs, or for a better job than that held at present, rejections are inevitable. It is very hard not to be discouraged. No one is alone in receiving rejections — they come to almost all unemployed people.

It can be extra disappointing if the interviewers are charming to the applicant, and creates the impression that he has a good chance of success. Perhaps they genuinely found it hard to choose between suitable candidates, or maybe more suitable candidates were interviewed later, so they changed their minds. The applicant must try not to feel personally rejected; it may well not have been the right job.

The important thing is to press on and continue making applications. Jobsearching needs courage, determination and perseverance. These are just the qualities many disabled people develop, and will probably be able to apply them to their search for a job. They could give an edge over non-disabled candidates. Keep looking and applying.

Starting a business

There are various schemes and organisations that could help anyone wishing to start up a business. Most of these, and some of the advantages and disadvantages of starting a business, are discussed in Chapter 8, which also contains points to watch, advice on efficiency, and suggests sources of further information.

In this section of the book I would especially mention Livewire, a scheme sponsored by Shell UK to encourage and support young people aged 16 to 25 'attempting to develop projects which can help them create their own work'. Details of the scheme are available from Livewire.

The scheme offers:

- An introduction to a local adviser who can talk through the idea and suggest the next steps
- Regional awards of cash, free publicity, training, equipment or premises to those who submit convincing action plans
- A chance to enter for the national awards.

Among the 1984-5 winners were:

- Two young men who set up a co-operative, Basta Pasta, making fresh pasta products for sale to the public and local restaurants
- A young couple who produced colourfully printed fabrics and plastic cushions
- A young man who is a small person, only 2 feet 6 inches tall, who began growing pot plants to sell. Despite hostility from some market traders, he was eventually allowed to use the end of one trader's stall. Now he has obtained

his own stall which he can stock as he can grow more plants because of his success in the Livewire scheme.

The Livewire booklet is realistic with amusing drawings that emphasise the hazards of starting one's own business, as well as the satisfaction to be gained.

Sending for the booklet is an important first step for any young person thinking of starting a business. It lists bodies such as Youth Enterprise Scheme (YES) and the Prince's Trust/ Jubilee Trust's 'Youth Business Initiative' which provide loans or bursaries for young unemployed people.

The Industrial Society, in conjunction with Midland Bank plc have produced a leaflet giving all the sources of help and advice which are available to young people going into business or considering self-employment. Copies are available from Enterprise Unit, Robert Hyde House, 48 Bryanston Square, London W1H 7LN; phone 01-262 2401.

Chapter 4

Looking for Advice on Careers and Employment

Sources of advice and help and special schemes such as 'Opportunities for the Disabled' are described in this chapter. As well as official services and schemes, informal ways of seeking jobs are mentioned, and there are suggestions on making a hobby or leisure interest a step to employment or earnings.

Statutory services

The Manpower Services Commission (MSC) is the body responsible for helping people find work, training, or temporary employment. Its activities include the Youth Training Scheme, adult training courses, Jobcentres, Community Programmes, the Enterprise Allowance Scheme (for helping people set up their own businesses), the Disablement Resettlement Service, and Professional and Executive Recruitment (known as PER).

Jobcentres

Jobcentres are mentioned frequently throughout this book. One of their advantages is that they offer self-service. Job searchers can read all the cards displayed and decide for themselves whether they would like to apply for any of the jobs described. It is not a case of someone else picking out the jobs they think would be suitable for disabled people. The disabled can choose from exactly the same selection as anybody else. In 1984-85 a total of 72,000 disabled people found work through Jobcentre services.

At the Jobcentre, a good range of MSC leaflets including the Jobhunting pack and 'Getting Back to Work' leaflet should be available.

Professional and Executive Recruitment (PER)

PER helps all professional and executive jobseekers, and their services are as appropriate for disabled executives as for able-bodied unemployed people. One of PER's most useful tools is *Executive Post*, a free weekly 40 page newspaper containing hundreds of job vacancies in every issue. As well as the display advertisements, there are jobs classified under such headings as General Management, Financial and Administrative, Personnel, Training and Education, Production Management, Technical Authors, and Welfare and Social Work. There is also a large section, arranged geographically, of MSC Special Programme vacancies for various occupations. The priorities given to disabled people are clearly set out.

Every issue contains helpful articles and hints on jobseeking, and frequently readers relate personal stories of their struggles to find employment.

DROs or Jobcentre staff will advise on eligibility for PER and supply the address of the nearest local PER office (there are about 37 in the UK). Someone who is not qualified for the register may have a friend who is on it, who would pass on a copy of *Executive Post*; it may be available in a public library reading room. Even if the jobs advertised in this paper are not suitable, the articles would be of help.

The booklet, 'Executive job-hunting for people with health problems or disability', is available from PER Head Office.

Job Training Schemes

The MSC Training Division will give advice on the Job Training Schemes and courses sponsored by the MSC. These courses are intended to equip people with better skills or teach them new skills. Disabled people are given special consideration when they apply for these courses, and eligibility rules may be relaxed for them. Look for the leaflet ATL 49, or later versions, in Jobcentres, or contact the nearest MSC Training Services Division.

The Bridge Programme, designed exclusively for executives and professionals, operates in most areas. It offers part-time courses that last up to four months and provide counselling and tuition in all aspects of jobhunting. Local Training Services Division Offices will supply details.

There is further information about training courses in the next chapter.

Local authority help

Some local authorities run their own schemes for advising disabled people who are having difficulty in finding the right job. As these schemes vary, seem to change constantly, close, and then new projects start, it will be necessary to find out what is available in each area. Ask the Town Hall information services, local Social Services, the Citizens' Advice Bureau, social workers, and other disabled people for news and information.

It is surprising how often officials do not seem to know about all the local schemes. It is no use waiting for someone to come along and tell you what is on offer; do your own research and ask friends to look out for you.

In a library I found a leaflet about a local 'Worklink' which is designed 'to enable people with disabilities to explore and develop their work abilities'. It also encourages 'local employers to widen the range of jobs for disabled people'. This scheme sounds most helpful, and if something similar is started in your area, do consider making use of it. When worthwhile schemes are started, it is important that disabled people should take advantage of them and tell others about them. If there is little response from disabled people, local councils could argue that there is 'no demand'. When a scheme meets a real need, use it and encourage others to do so. If you think the wrong type of provision is being made, say so. Make your reactions known to a local councillor or to the organisation concerned.

Opportunities for the Disabled

This organisation was established in 1980 by a group of leading employers who had recognised the need for co-ordinated action to ensure that disabled jobseekers received a fair chance of open employment.

Two main services are provided, both free of charge. The first aims to improve the employment prospects for people with disabilities and help them get real jobs. The second provides a service to employers, and offers them guidance on the financial assistance and aids available if they take on disabled employees.

Opportunities for the Disabled has 10 local offices in cities such as Bristol, Birmingham, Leicester, Manchester, Hull, and Sheffield, which disabled people seeking employment can contact for help. Some jobseekers hear about the service through friends and contacts in organisations for the disabled, some through DROs. Anyone can telephone the London Headquarters on 01-726 4961, and ask for the address of the nearest office.

Staff at the Opportunities for the Disabled offices try to help people find jobs on a 'match-up' basis. They have contacts with local employers who support the organisation and want to help.

Since the service started, all kinds of disabled people have been guided into employment. There is Christine, a small person, who irons leather at a leather goods firm in Leicestershire; Tim, who is a little slow since suffering a road accident but works happily filling shelves for Woolworths; Charles, a skilled draughtsman who lost his sight and then retrained as a switchboard telephonist, and who now operates a switchboard with 18 outside lines and 85 extensions; and two deaf girls who work on word processors at the Bank of England.

In addition, some large firms have given services or equipment, such as the Optacon machine, donated by Citibank, that allows specially trained blind people to read ordinary print; the LEVO Chair, donated by Dalgety; and the keyboard skills courses, donated by Sight and Sound, for deaf pupils.

Other companies, including Marks and Spencer, Access, ICI, Wimpey, the London Electricity Board, and Barclays Bank, have seconded professional staff, or made premises available for the service.

'Employers don't just talk about offering opportunities for the disabled, they make them', is the slogan adopted by the organisation.

Association of Graduate Careers Advisory Service

This service has been set up to collect information about disabled graduates and their work. It aims to provide data on how disabilities have been overcome in a wide variety of occupations. To enrich the information in their data bank the Association invites disabled graduates to tell it about their experience.

To help disabled graduates who are seeking employment, the data bank is willing to supply employers with information about the ways in which disabled people have overcome problems. Any graduates who are willing to contribute their experience, or who are in need of advice, should contact the Disabled Graduates Data Bank Careers Advisory Service.

Publications

In addition to *Executive Post*, there are other publications particularly aimed at the jobhunter. These include: *Employment News*, which contains news of courses and new job initiatives; local employment papers, and *Graduate Post*. When looking for a job, it is advisable to study a wide range of publications:

- Local papers, including those for the surrounding area as well as the immediate area
- National papers; on certain days they carry advertisements for particular fields: for instance, on Mondays the *Guardian* has pages of Secretarial, Creative and Media posts.
- Trade and technical papers
- Consumer magazines, such as *The Lady*, that carry job vacancy advertisements
- Magazines related to particular interests, for instance the religious papers with situations vacant columns.

It is possible for disabled people to keep and exchange papers and magazines with others, as well as looking at copies in libraries, day centres and clubs.

Exhibitions

Occasionally there are large exhibitions aimed at bringing together jobhunters and employers. Although they may not make any special effort to serve disabled people, such exhibitions could be useful to those who are mobile enough to visit them. One may meet an employer who had not previously thought of recruiting a disabled person. Be well informed about the grants for modifications and adaptations, and MSC schemes to help an employer who takes on a disabled person, and perhaps carry some of the relevant leaflets. The employers need to see the enthusiasm disabled people have to offer, and hear about their training and experience. The applicant may have to settle for being taken on for a trial period; that is quite usual. The important thing is having a chance to show what he or she can do. Many able-bodied people are on an initial six months' trial when taking up a post with a new employer.

Seminars

PER runs regular one-day seminars for unemployed people

seeking professional, executive, technical and scientific jobs. They are held at over 30 different towns from Aberdeen to Woking, and reasonable travelling expenses are reimbursed for those who attend their nearest seminar but still need to travel at least four miles. These seminars offer talks, counselling sessions and an opportunity to meet other jobhunters. Seminar application forms appear in *Executive Post*.

Look out for any other talks, lectures or courses arranged locally for unemployed people.

Organisations for disabled people could lay on a study day, a series of talks, a lecture on jobseeking, or ask disabled people to come and tell members about their jobs and careers, how they started in them, and what advice they would give to others. The Association of Disabled Professionals may be able to provide a speaker (whose travelling expenses would need to be reimbursed).

Among themselves disabled people have a wealth of knowledge about disability, problems and solutions. In a discussion every disabled person would have something to contribute; it is useful to hear about negative experiences as well as successes. If problems are brought out into the open, able-bodied people, local authorities and social workers may develop new understanding of what it is like to be disabled.

Anyone who has been to a special school or college, attended a course or rehabilitation centre, should take every opportunity of telling the organisers what was helpful and positive, and how improvements should be made. Sometimes it takes courage to speak up, but there is no need for disabled people to be passive consumers. Charities, local councils and central government spend a great deal of money on services for disabled people. Sometimes it seems as if they should be more ready to consult disabled people and ask them what they think is needed. Services that make it easier for a disabled person to find and keep employment would surely have high priority as far as most disabled people of working age are concerned.

Radio and television

London's Capital Radio and other local stations often advertise specific vacancies over the air. Listen to your local radio station and use it. When there are phone-in programmes take part; seize every opportunity to make it known that there are disabled people looking for work — you never know who may be listening and feel prompted to reply.

Study the schedules and make a point of listening or watching when there are programmes on careers and employment. Open University and schools programmes may be particularly useful.

TV aid to job-finding

A Ceefax style job-finding service has been set up experimentally in the Midlands. After normal broadcasting ends viewers can tune into a Central TV programme which brings local vacancies and training courses to the screen with a reference number. Viewers simply note the reference number of the vacancy that appeals to them and then ask their local Jobcentre for more details.

Use leisure interests

Whatever their interests, sport or hobby, disabled people should consider whether they would offer any chance of employment. Suggestions for starting one's own business based on a hobby are contained in Chapter 8, and in Chapter 12 there is more information on leisure activities that could lead to earnings. But it is worth considering employment and careers too.

Perhaps the activity has an organisation, governing body, educational service or promotional council that employs office staff. If so, could an opening be found there? Keen members of a political party could find out if staff are needed in a local office.

Is there any work that avid readers could do in the local library? What about the story-telling sessions that some libraries run for children? Would a library consider starting such a service experimentally, and allow a disabled person to organise it and read? Does any local association for blind people know of visually handicapped students who need readers?

Does a local sports centre need administrative or coaching staff? SportsJobs for disabled people was the imaginative theme of a 1984 conference organised by Opportunities for the Disabled. A blind film producer gave a talk, 'Fit for Sport means Fit for Work', and urged the audience: 'We must all have a crack at the jobs in the growing sports industries and associations.' Disabled people could use the knowledge, skill, and confidence they have gained in sport to help them when they are looking for a job or career.

A disabled person who thoroughly enjoys driving and is

highly skilled could test him or herself by taking the Institute of Advanced Motorists' test. Perhaps they could then train as a driving instructor and specialise in teaching disabled people. You will know how much life can be transformed by being able to drive, and could encourage disabled people to persevere with learning — if it seems wise for them.

Perhaps there is a magazine concerned with your hobby. Does it need contributors, office staff, or advertisement sales representatives? Are there shops selling equipment needed for the hobby? Would they like to employ a well-informed sales assistant?

I could go on giving examples and making suggestions, but there is no need. Every disabled person could think out for himself: 'Is there any way in which my hobby could lead to employment?'

Friends and contacts

For everyone, able-bodied or disabled, obtaining a job, a lucky break, an unexpected chance of earning, often comes through knowing someone, from being in the right place at the right time, from being alert and ready to take opportunities. As a disabled person, whether or not you are seeking work, it is enriching to have plenty of friends from a wide variety of backgrounds and careers, of both sexes and from different age-groups. This can be difficult to achieve for those who have lived a rather sheltered life and attended special schools and colleges, so it is important to take every opportunity for getting to know more people. Churches, clubs and societies, classes, tenants or residents associations, parent/teacher organisations, political and environmental groups, can all be sources of contacts and friendships.

If you are disabled, talk to your friends; tell them about your desire to find a career or interesting job. Each one of them will have his or her own circle of contacts, so through your friends more people are likely to hear about you, and think of you when a vacancy comes along.

You may know other people who are also looking for a career or job. Help each other; pass on hints, and exchange ideas. Share your good news and encourage one another. If you get a job first, don't forget the other people who shared your plight. Most of us have cause to be grateful to some individual who has encouraged us or given us an opportunity.

Remember the help you have received, and try to help at least one other person.

Organisations

Some disabled people may not want to be active in organisations for the disabled because they do not wish to be labelled 'disabled', but it can be worth contacting this sort of organisation for advice and literature on finding employment.

Also, disabled people can be of help to such organisations as they often make representations to the All Party Disablement Group. This is a group of MPs and peers who take a special interest in issues concerning disabled people, and support legislation for their welfare.

Personal experience and suggestions for improvements in services and opportunities may well be of help to an organisation preparing evidence to put before the Group.

Private employment agencies

Disabled people should contact some of the local employment agencies and branches of national employment bureaux to see what they have to offer in permanent, temporary or occasional work. Tell them what you are able to do and about any services, such as word processing or envelope stuffing, you are able to offer at home.

Try to build up a good relationship with a sympathetic interviewer, and make sure you acquire a reputation for doing thorough, efficient work. You want the agency to call on you often because you are reliable person — not because they are sorry for you.

Even if you do not feel able to work permanently, you may have a skill, such as being able to work a switchboard, that you could use in temporary relief jobs.

Look in the Yellow Pages for addresses of local agencies and note any that specialise in relevant age groups, or types of work. *Do not pay any fees* — reputable agencies charge the employer, not the staff. Check that the agency is registered with the local authority; most registered agencies display their registration certificate prominently.

Local action groups

Look around your neighbourhood and see if there are any

groups concerned about the problem of local unemployment and the people involved. In some places there are counsellors who help newly redundant people through the shock and grief redundancy can cause.

Some churches run resource centres for unemployed people; others set up workshops, initiate Community Programmes or open volunteer bureaux to put unemployed people in touch with local projects needing voluntary help.

If you are unemployed, take advantage of any services or action groups that seem likely to be helpful. Just talking to other unemployed people may be useful, and it is important to think through the whole question of work, and what should be one's attitude towards it, now that fewer people can expect to spend the greater part of their lives in full-time work.

New moves

In order to help people who have been unemployed for a long time, the MSC is experimenting with some new methods of giving help and advice. In pilot areas some unemployed people are being invited to come to Jobcentres for interviews where their situation and prospects will be discussed in depth, and advice given.

Job clubs are being started; at these, unemployed people will have easy access to telephones and the stationery they need for job applications.

There are also financial benefits, with weekly allowances being offered to long-term unemployed people who take poorly paid jobs, and more loans for small businesses.

However keen he is to get a job, a disabled person should think carefully before taking one that is very poorly paid, or dull. One rehabilitation worker told me: 'When people have been ill or have suffered disablement, they want work that is stimulating, creative, or makes them feel needed. It isn't enough just to be working — it must seem to be work worth doing.' She mentioned Marie who had been unemployed after a mental illness, but now worked happily as a craft therapy aide in an old people's home.

Chapter 5

Education and Training Opportunities

Introduction

This chapter describes training and education opportunities that could be explored by people with disabilities.

Some of the centres mentioned, such as Training Workshops and residential colleges, offer specialised courses for disabled people, and schemes, run by charities and organisations, that are specifically intended for people with disabilities, but the chapter also looks at all types of educational institutions.

Studying at a further education college, 'second chance' college, private college, adult education institute, or university is encouraged, and sources of further information are given. There is also a brief description of the work of the National Bureau for Handicapped Students.

Readers are urged to consider distance learning through correspondence courses, and especially the Open University. They are recommended to find out more about the OU services for students with disabilities, 2000 of whom are at present studying with the OU to improve career prospects or for the pleasure, achievement, and widening of experience and interest that such study brings.

The availability of aids for studying is mentioned, with sources of further information, and the grant position is discussed with suggestions on obtaining discretionary help from voluntary bodies.

The whole chapter stresses the importance of accepting opportunities for training, and the wisdom of using spare time for learning and personal development.

Special schemes

Training for disabled people who are keen to work is offered by a number of bodies: government, local authority and voluntary. Ask your careers officer or Jobcentre to tell you about the possibilities, but do your own research too. You may want to:

- Add to your general education
- Prepare for a profession
- Acquire a new skill
- Develop and update your existing skills or professional training.

MSC Training Division

The Training Services Agency of the MSC aims to provide training to meet the needs of individuals, and it also caters for the special training needs of disabled people. While many disabled men and women are able to train alongside non-disabled people in Training Services Agency Skillcentres, further education colleges, private and voluntary colleges, on specialist short courses of perhaps four or eight weeks, or with employers, others are glad to take advantage of the four existing residential training colleges.

The four colleges, Finchale Training College, Durham; Portland Training College, Mansfield; Queen Elizabeth's Training College, Leatherhead; and St Loye's College, Exeter, offer a great variety of subjects and skills, and new courses are always being added to keep in line with current employment opportunities. Some courses at Queen Elizabeth's Training College are specially designed for school-leavers.

Going away to a residential college can demand a lot of courage if you are disabled, but it can be well worth making the effort. Young people who go to these colleges gain in independence and self-reliance. As well as getting to know different people and learning new skills, all those who go to the colleges discover some of the employment possibilities that will be open to them after training.

About 900 disabled people complete these residential training courses each year, and most of them subsequently obtain jobs. Applications for a place at one of these colleges should be made through a Jobcentre DRO or a Specialist Careers Officer.

Full information about residential training colleges can be obtained from a DRO or an Employment Rehabilitation Centre. MSC leaflet TSA L65 (or later versions), 'Residential Training for Disabled People', gives full details about the organisation of the colleges, financial arrangements, and courses offered.

Training Workshops

Many Training Workshops are not specially dedicated to the needs of disabled people, but they do make provision so that young disabled people can become trainees alongside able-bodied people. This is the policy in London, which has 40 Training Workshops sponsored by local authorities, projects and charities within the Youth Training Scheme.

Between them these workshops teach a great many skills, including design, photography, woodwork, computer use, knitwear/textile design and silk-screen printing. As part of the course, trainees are offered work experience placements. All the workshops are individually organised with their own pattern of courses and placements. A disabled person needs to look around and see which courses would be most useful and accessible.

There is a *Directory of London Training Workshops 1985-86* which careers officers or DROs are likely to have. Ask if you can look through it with them, and discuss which courses might be suitable for you. Alternatively, ask the Training Workshops Resource Unit for the addresses of local workshops.

Residential colleges

Apart from the four residential colleges already mentioned, there are a number of other residential colleges especially for disabled students. Most of these are run by voluntary bodies, and many are mainly for young people. They include:

Nash House, Hayes, Kent, a small residential unit, attached to Coney Hill School, which offers independence courses that include typing and home economics. The school and unit are run by the Shaftesbury Society.

National Star Centre for Disabled Youth, Ullenwood Manor, Cheltenham, which takes 120 students who follow general education courses. Contact the Principal for the prospectus.

Lord Mayor Treloar College, Alton, Hampshire, run by the Treloar Trust. This college has excellent sporting facilities and offers general education as well as vocational training for young disabled people.

Beaumont College of Further Education, which is run by the Spastics Society, offers a two year course for about 100 residential students and a few day students. Most of the students here have severe physical handicaps and though many of them have attended special day and boarding schools, or ordinary schools, their physical disabilities have often hindered their learning. At Beaumont the aim is to help students develop personal and social maturity, basic skills and 'satisfying and relevant' occupational skills. Application forms may be obtained from the Principal.

Derwen Training College for the Disabled, Oswestry, provides assessment and vocational training in a great variety of fields. Students can attend vocational courses in local further education colleges, and this means that a wide variety of options is open to them. Courses suggested include: leatherwork; dressmaking and soft furnishings; and shoemaking and repairing. The college has a voluntary board of governors. Students attending the college need to be sponsored by their local education authority or Social Services office.

Sherrards Training Centre, Digswell Hill, Welwyn, provides assessment and training in electrical and mechanical assembly, packing, light engineering and woodwork. It aims to prepare people with cerebral palsy, and those with other handicaps, for suitable open or sheltered employment. Trainees normally stay at the centre for six to 12 months. The Centre's careers officer gives advice on future employment, and works in co-operation with the trainee's local careers officer or DRO.

Hereward College in Coventry offers a variety of courses. It is run by Coventry Education Authority but students, sponsored by their own local education authority, come to it from all parts of the UK. The courses are organised in conjunction with the local further education college, and students can prepare for higher education or skilled employment. Computer and information technology courses have enabled past students to find work they can do at home or in offices.

It is a great advantage that this college is so closely linked with an ordinary further education college and it means that students have a chance to enjoy plenty of social life as well as benefiting from the special facilities and adaptations that make life easier for people in wheelchairs. Application forms and further information can be obtained from the college Admissions Officer. Early application is advised.

Other residential training

There are a number of other smaller colleges and units offering vocational training and preparation for independent living. Lists are included in the Queen Elizabeth's Foundation *Directory* (see page 38). You can also obtain information from: Dr Barnardo's; The National Children's Home; The Church of England Children's Society; Mencap Pathway; RADAR; Association for Spina Bifida and Hydrocephalus; The Spastics Society; and the Grange School of Stitchery and Lace, Bookham, Surrey.

As well as consulting DROs and careers officers, disabled young people, their advisers, and parents could make contact with these and other organisations, and see what specialist provision is available.

It may be hard to allow a young disabled person to go away from home, but it is important to think of the future. Going away to a specialist college may be the best way to learn independence and prepare for a career.

There are many opportunities especially for young people and it is as well to take advantage of these while the disabled person is young enough. If young people have the chance of going away on a course, help them to prepare for it by learning to do as much as possible for themselves.

In the Children's Society communal living units for severely physically handicapped children, I have met disabled youngsters who have never even made a cup of tea for themselves while living at home or in an institution. Some have never washed their own hair or looked after their own clothes. Yet, with the example of others, encouragement and perseverance, they have gained a large measure of independence. For anyone who has lived at home with caring parents, going away from home or a protective institution is bound to be a shock. Try to soften it by preparing yourself or your child.

When you are considering applying for a place at a residential college, try to visit it beforehand. If it is offered, take the chance of a short, experimental stay; ask if you can meet a former student — or at least telephone one for a chat. But don't be put off by one person's experience. What is 'disastrous' for one may be 'the best thing I ever did' for another. Going to a residential college can be the first step towards achieving a satisfying and rewarding career.

The National Bureau for Handicapped Students is always glad to give advice to deaf and hard of hearing students and potential students. There are many technological advances that should make it easier for deaf students to study with hearing students. To keep abreast of current developments, such as keyboards linked with telephones, electronic mail, and computers that turn speech into the printed word, order *Soundbarrier*, the journal of the Royal National Institute for the Deaf (RNID).

Sound barriers

The Royal National Institute for the Deaf can supply information on training courses designed for deaf people. Those who live in or near London are fortunate as the City Lit Centre for the Deaf offers a wide range of courses as part of the Inner London Education Authority (ILEA) services for the hearing impaired in adult, further and higher education; there is also speech and language therapy for adults.

Courses include Vocational Preparation offering keyboard skills, technical drawing, computing, engineering, and other subjects. There is also a Turning Point course for deaf people over 21 who are unemployed; this provides training in clerical skills or preparation for more advanced study and leads to nationally recognised examinations. At present (September 1986) it runs for three days a week, 10.30 – 4.30.

Those who are fluent in signing can train to become teachers of signing. There are education and career counsellors based at the Centre, and special help is offered to deaf and hard of hearing Open University students, and also to those at higher education colleges in the ILEA, and on Youth Training Schemes.

If you want to improve your speech, lipreading, use of hearing aids or communication skills, it is well worth finding out about all the courses offered. Information is available from the Centre for Deaf and Speech Therapy. For courses beginning in September it is necessary to apply to the Admissions Officer by the previous 31 January.

The Royal National Institute for the Deaf considers that employment, unemployment and underemployment are priority issues; they welcome the Vocational Preparation course and hope it will encourage other local education authorities to set up similar courses.

For students living in Inner London, fees at the City Lit are very reasonable, while those living in the outer London boroughs and home counties pay a little more. Other students can obtain help from their own local education authority. It is not a good idea to give a fraudulent address to obtain a reduction in fees; this is bound to be discovered and may lead to prosecution and exclusion from the courses.

Training for visually handicapped people

The Royal National Institute for the Blind
The RNIB, founded in 1868, helps visually handicapped school-leavers who are looking for employment. It also tries to find jobs for adults who have visual handicaps.

The Institute has an employment service that passes on to employers information about work methods and equipment that can be used by blind people and it advises on obtaining financial assistance with the cost of using a reader.

At the RNIB's Commercial Training College in London, selected students are trained 'to the highest standards to ensure that they can compete for jobs on equal terms with sighted people'. Courses offered include audio typing, word processing, switchboard operating and computer programming.

After training, some blind people are able to use the Optacon — a portable machine which enables a person to feel and identify print. Erica, a student from the college, described how she demonstrated her skills at a Birmingham/International Business Show.

'I felt honoured that I should be chosen to represent the college at the show — along with two other final year students. I joined Tony, confined to a wheelchair but a brilliant engineer; Jane, with cerebral palsy, who has nevertheless overcome her speed and co-ordination difficulties and is a chartered accountant with IBM computers, and another Jane, a victim of a motor cycle accident that led to complete paralysis of the right forearm, who works as a secretary typing at 45 words a minute with one hand.

'I somehow felt apprehensive. Would I be able to demonstrate to all those people what we were trying to get across in our stand for opportunities for the disabled? We wanted to show that disabled applicants, given the same chances as everyone else, can make efficient and confident employees.

'A number of people said to me: "That's an ordinary typewriter you are using isn't it?" because I did quite a lot of typing, as well as reading with the Optacon. It was tiring, but extremely interesting meeting so many people . . . any scheme such as this can only help in making us feel equals among our so-called able-bodied competitors when searching for the jobs which are now becoming more elusive every day.'*

The RNIB produces excellent booklets setting out the training
* With acknowledgement to *Opportunities for the Disabled*.

facilities for blind people and giving examples of the work that blind people do. Courses offered include audio typing, word processing, switchboard operating and computer programming. The fees for these courses are generally met by the MSC Training Division.

The RNIB also has a Rehabilitation Centre where people who have lost their sight learn to adjust to their new condition and organise their daily living. There are two main types of course: social rehabilitation and vocational rehabilitation. Applications for vocational courses should be made through the Employment Division of the MSC. Details are available from Jobcentres.

The vocational course aims to help students decide what would be the most suitable employment for them. It provides an introduction to office work, and the Centre has a large range of modern aids including talking computer terminals, printers, talking calculators, and closed circuit televisions which magnify print on to their screens. The Industrial Department gives students experience in basic machine operating and assembly work.

Since 1895 blind students have been trained in massage, and this work has developed so that now visually handicapped students are prepared for the normal Membership of the Chartered Society of Physiotherapy. The course for visually handicapped physiotherapists is based at the Whittington Hospital in Highgate, and is administered by the RNIB.

Candidates for the course should have a visual handicap sufficient to prevent them from training in a sighted school, but they cannot be accepted if they have a second disability. They need to be mobile, independent, have a knowledge of braille, and be able to touch-type. Since 1915 more than 800 students have qualified at the school. Application forms can be obtained from the North London School of Physiotherapy.

According to *The Advocate*, the journal of the National League of the Blind and Disabled, the RNIB spent over £800,000 on employment services in 1984-85. They helped blind people to find jobs, prepare for jobs in modern offices, and set up their own business.

Catching up on O and A levels

While you are unemployed, searching for a job or course,

recovering from an accident or undergoing a period of treatment, you may have spare time you could put to good use. Perhaps you want to obtain an academic qualification, learn a new skill, or improve your qualifications. An extra O or A level could make a difference to your curriculum vitae (CV). It will show you still have the ability to study, and are able to get into the routine of studying once again.

Attending classes will take you out of the house and into contact with a group of ordinary able-bodied people. You are the person to decide whether or not you would be able to attend a local further education college. Find out about part-time day and evening O and A level courses at these colleges. Alternatively, there may be an Evening Institute that has afternoon courses.

Correspondence courses

There is also the possibility of doing all kinds of courses by correspondence. This will bring you less personal contact, but will still be useful and provide an interest as well as getting you into the habit of studying regularly and methodically.

Having reading and writing to do can be a distraction when you are in pain or discomfort, or when you are tempted to feel depressed. Send to the National Extension College, 18 Brooklands Avenue, Cambridge CB2 2HN, for the Home Learning Catalogue of Correspondence Courses. The College offers a wide variety of O and A level, business and technology courses. There are also non-examination courses, such as successful play-writing. Taking one of these courses can be a way of widening your interests and of stimulating mental activity. The NEC is just one of the 37 colleges approved by the Council for the Accreditation of Correspondence Colleges. A list is obtainable from CACC.

Voluntary organisation courses

Some voluntary organisations run training courses at centres that are recognised as further education establishments. For instance, there are religious colleges, such as the New Hope Bible College in Scotland, that accept people who have been unemployed for at least three months. While studying there, students are eligible to continue receiving unemployment and any incapacity benefits that they have been receiving during the previous three months. This intensive course is primarily concerned with evangelism, but basic training in workplace skills is offered alongside Biblical and religious studies. However, it is only suitable for 'Born again Christians'. Another Christian training centre where the DHSS provides board, lodging and pocket money, is the Haven Christian Training Centre at 1 Westgate Hill, Pembroke, Dyfed. Your minister may know of others.

Further education colleges

Further education colleges, sometimes called technical colleges, colleges of commerce, or similar titles, are run by local authorities in almost every major town in Britain. They offer a wide variety of courses for the over-16s. Your local library will have a list of courses, or a careers officer will be able to advise you. At most of these colleges, courses begin in September of each year, and as late entrants are not accepted it is vital to plan and apply for a place in good time.

Tuition is free for the under-18s but fees are charged for the over-18s. Local authorities can give discretionary awards to help cover these fees. If you decide to take a course at this sort of college, watch your benefit position and check with your local DHSS Office or DRO.

Many colleges of further education are modern buildings with good provision for disabled students.

Private colleges

If you are particularly keen to take an intensive course, to study a vocational subject such as cookery, floristry or the decorative arts, or to be in a small group of students, you may decide to go to a private college even though it is likely to be expensive. This could also be the choice for those keen to do a secretarial or computing course, or anyone in need of a sheltered environment. Look in local papers, and study directories of private colleges to find somewhere that is well-established. You need to check that the course or the training that is offered will prepare you for a recognised examination.

West Dean College

This college offers courses in the restoration of antique ceramics and porcelain, restoration of antique furniture, making of early musical instruments, and in the restoration of antique clocks. The courses are recognised by the British Accreditation Council for Independent Further and Higher Education. The Principal wrote to me: 'I am pleased to say that we are, with our Trustees, planning to make extensive alterations within the house to provide a lift and a limited number of bedrooms for disabled people in wheelchairs so that they might be able to undertake our short courses. The MSC have, for many years, made special provision to provide grants for disabled students to undertake our one-year restoration courses. Antique clock restoration seems to attract a number of men who have received industrial injuries, who have engineering skills and want to develop a career that has little requirement for mobility.'

Further information about the courses at West Dean is available from the Principal.

Literacy courses

One DRO pointed out to me that people who have been engaged in manual work for many years, and then suffered an injury which prevents them from continuing with manual work, sometimes find that they have lost their literacy skills and are out of practice with simple mathematics. In such circumstances, she suggests that they take a literacy course to polish up these skills and improve their chances of obtaining new work.

If you wish to take a literacy course, look in your public library for lists of local places where such courses are available. You will also find information about literacy courses at community centres, in some post offices, and displayed in public buildings.

Part-time and full-time degree courses

Many colleges and universities are now offering part-time day degree courses in a variety of subjects. A disabled person with mobility or fitness problems may find such a course possible when a full-time degree course would be too demanding.

If you are considering a part-time or a full-time degree course, make enquiries at local polytechnics, institutes of higher education, education colleges, and local university colleges. It would also be wise to consult the National Bureau for Handicapped students, especially when going away from home to study.

Some universities and colleges may be willing to waive formal entry requirements for candidates with maturity and experience. A full list of all UK universities, colleges, and courses available is contained in the UCCA Handbook, *How to apply for admission to a university*, available from The Universities Central Council on Admissions. Some colleges have better facilities than others for disabled people, who should try to look at several places before applying. One graduate told me that she studied on a modern campus that had six main buildings without lifts. As she is confined to a wheelchair this had its difficulties for her, but she obtained her degree, and is now doing administrative work in an organisation for the disabled.

The General Synod Board of Education will send a list of all the Church Education Colleges. These are former Teacher Training Colleges but nowadays they prepare students for various types of work with children, and in the arts. Roman Catholics should ask their parish priest about the Catholic colleges.

Finding a course

Those who have difficulty in finding a suitable course may want to consult Educational Guidance Services for Adults. To enquire about the nearest EGSA, telephone 0908 368924. This body offers free and independent educational guidance on courses and admission requirements, and is not linked to any particular educational institution. Advice is also given on grants.

CRAC Directories of Further Education and Graduate Studies are generally available in libraries. CRAC will send a brochure on request. It is also useful to consult *British Qualifications*, published by Kogan Page. These directories are updated every year, so if you look at a library copy, check that it is the most recent available.

A free directory of first degree courses is available from: The Publications Officer, Council for National Academic Awards. An information leaflet giving details of all degree and other advanced courses within the Central Register and Clearing House scheme is available, free of charge. Remember also to contact the National Bureau for Handicapped Students, and ask for their notes and advice for disabled applicants.

Open University

Whether it is to improve your career prospects, for the satisfaction of achieving a degree, or for the pleasure studying brings you, study with the Open University is an option that anyone who is unable to work could well consider.

Study is carried out at home through correspondence, reading, listening to radio and watching Open University TV programmes. Students have personal tutors who set and mark work and offer advice; summer schools and tutorial weekends give students a chance to meet their tutors and other students and join in discussion, thus overcoming the feeling of isolation sometimes experienced by those who undertake 'distance learning'.

It would be a creative way of using the spare time you have as a disabled person who is temporarily or permanently unemployed. As it says in the brochure: 'An Open University degree could make a big difference to your future . . . '

You do not need to have O or A levels to begin studying with the OU, but you need to be aged 18 or over, live in the UK, have a determination to succeed and an appetite for hard work.

Since the scheme started 17 years ago, some 75,711 people have gained OU degrees, new hope, confidence, and better career prospects. The subjects offered number 125. For a full list write to the Open University.

Students with disabilities receive special support when they study with the OU which has an exceptionally large number of disabled students.

One unit, the Office for Students with Disabilities, co-ordinates the special services. For visually handicapped students there are audio tapes of course material, and deaf students are given transcripts of radio programmes. Weekend induction courses are arranged for visually handicapped and deaf students. Those unable to travel are allowed to take examinations at home. Write for detailed information on the support available.

In addition to the degree courses, there are single, self-contained courses that can be studied for personal interest, the understanding of new technology, or for practical help with everyday life. In some places, such as community centres, small groups work together on these courses. The single courses are part of an Associate Student Programme, and full information can be obtained by writing to: PO Box 76, The Open University, Walton Hall, Milton Keynes MK7 6AN.

Open BTEC

The MSC is now sponsoring a new business studies distance learning scheme for working people at junior management level who cannot fit into a timetable of day release, block release or evening courses.

Cassette tapes and videos, as well as books, are used and it is expected that students will study mainly on their own at a time and place to suit themselves. The courses are designed to help those who have been away from study for some time, or who have not been able to follow other study programmes.

It seems as if they would be suitable for a disabled person who has had managerial experience; students must be over 21 and have had three years' work experience. For further details contact the Business and Technician Education Council.

Adult residential colleges

There are about eight adult residential colleges, mostly started by pioneers who wanted to provide an introduction to higher education for those who had left school early, or had been unable to attend school.

The same applies as for further education colleges: find out for yourself what these colleges are like; see if they offer courses that appeal to you; consider whether the building will be suitable for you, or if there are special facilities for disabled students.

You should be able to get your fees paid by your local education authority, and some of these colleges have their own bursary funds.

Though no formal entry qualifications are usually required, it does help if you can show you have been studying by correspondence or by attending local classes. You need to be capable academically of following the course offered.

Fircroft College in Birmingham, Hillcroft College (for women only) in Surbiton, Surrey, and Newbattle Abbey, Midlothian, are examples of these 'second chance' colleges.

The Co-operative College, Loughborough, has eight study bedrooms that can accommodate students in wheelchairs.

Adult education institutes

Most local authorities provide a number of adult education

institutes offering day and evening courses. Find out what is available in your area. Studying at one of these colleges provides a good opportunity for mixing with non-disabled people.

To take Lambeth as an example, it offers morning, afternoon, and evening classes in a tremendous variety of subjects. Here is a small selection: Basic Education, Computers, Keep Fit, Food Studies, Jazz Music, Metal Work and Jewellery, Basketry, and Weaving. There are crèche facilities at some institutes.

Peter, who is disabled through a motoring accident, told me how much he enjoyed going to an ordinary Keep Fit class where he took part in weight-lifting among other activities. He felt he had benefited socially and physically by joining in this class.

One member of the Association of Disabled Professionals recently described how he started attending a cookery evening class run by his local authority, but after the first night he decided he would not continue as access to the institute was so difficult for him. However, in a neighbouring local education authority a ramp was speedily built so that he could attend a class at one of their centres.

Morley College

In South London, Morley College has made great efforts to provide access for disabled students. A printed sheet, available from the college, gives details of the facilities that are accessible, width of doorways, lifts, and parking arrangements. Tutors there are briefed on assistance for disabled students in the case of fire. The new wing of the college, added in 1973, was planned with the needs of disabled people firmly in mind, but some of the classrooms in the older buildings have no lift access. To prevent disappointment, this is clearly stated in the notes. Students will appreciate the fact that the college has taken the trouble to state what are the realistic options for disabled people.

The National Bureau for Handicapped Students

The NBHS was set up in 1975 to expand and improve education, training and employment opportunities for young people and adults with special needs. It is concerned with people affected by any aspect of handicap — whether physical, sensory or learning difficulty — in further, higher and adult education. It aims to improve both the quality and quantity of post-school provisions for people with special needs. It is a voluntary body with limited resources, but it has helped many students by informing them of the grants to which they are entitled and by giving them skilled, individual advice that has enabled them to overcome problems and study successfully.

The Bureau offers:

- Information on work for young people being carried out by educational institutions, government agencies and voluntary organisations.
- Advice on admissions to colleges, specialist help, grants, examination arrangements and all that affects the welfare of students with special needs. The Bureau's advice service is open to prospective students, parents, careers officers, social workers and college staff.

An office block in Brixton, South London, made fully accessible to people with disabilities, is the Bureau's headquarters. Initial contact could be made by telephone or letter.

The organisation of personal care for students hoping to live independently in college, and the use of new technology for severely handicapped students, are the Bureau's current special concerns. It is also keen to offer more information and staff training so as to enable colleges to expand their services for students with special needs.

Those with queries about courses, accommodation, equipment and special provision for students should contact the Bureau.

Student aids

There are many microcomputer aids that can be of enormous help to deaf and visually handicapped students, and to those with limited physical dexterity, but these are expensive. The National Bureau for Handicapped Students administers a fund, sponsored by the *Sunday Times* and VNU Business Publishing and known as the Comet Scheme, that assists disabled students who want to purchase microcomputer equipment. There is also the Snowdon Award Scheme which helps to provide aids for disabled students. It is worth finding out from the NBHS if you would be eligible for help through these bodies.

You could also do some research for yourself, or for your child, to see if there are local charities with broad enough purposes to give a grant for purchase of an aid. Apart from educational charities, there are old parochial charities and trusts to which you could apply if you fulfil the age and residential qualifications.

Has your old school or college a benevolent fund that could help? Or is there a fund attached to the hospital where you may have received treatment? Ask the hospital social workers about this. Do you belong to an organisation that has a discretionary fund? Perhaps you were in a youth organisation that may be able to help you. If you worked before your accident, did you belong to a trade union that could assist you? Think about all aspects of your life, and see if there is a link somewhere with a charitable body or fund. You could consult the *Directory of Grant Making Trusts* which is available in larger public libraries and in the resource centres of voluntary bodies.

The government has now introduced funding to provide microelectronic equipment for disabled students in further education.

This provision is being made through the Educational Support Grant to local authorities, so the local education authority is the body to which students should apply for such grant aid. The sum allocated for this provision, for the period 1986-88, is £1 million. Details are contained in the Department of Education and Science Circular 5/85.

Mature students

An increasing proportion of older people are becoming university students. Though the number of undergraduates in total is decreasing, the number of mature students is increasing rapidly. Universities find that mature students are prepared to work hard and seriously, and they are less distracted by the sport and social life most colleges offer. An older person who has become disabled and is thinking of taking a degree course need not feel that he or she will be out of place because of being older than the average student. The UCCA booklet, 'Mature Students and Universities', emphasises that mature students are welcome 'because of their particular contribution to the life of a university'.

Birmingham Polytechnic has an 'Alternative Admission' course for mature people who want to study for a degree. The Admissions Tutor at your local polytechnic will be able to tell you whether they have started, or are planning, such a course.

Some areas, including Birmingham, have adult education advisory centres.

Applying for further education

When you apply for a course, do not meekly accept rejection because you are disabled. Point out how disabilities and the individual involved vary greatly. One person with a condition may be successful because of his or her determination, whereas another with similar disabilities may feel unable to tackle or continue a course.

Yvonne, born with cerebral palsy in 1946, went to a Spastics Society Home, where she met John who was also born with cerebral palsy. Like Yvonne, he was in a wheelchair, but as he had no handgrip he had to be fed. However, with a stick fastened to his forehead, John learnt to type. His speech was difficult to understand for those who did not know him well, but his mind was lively. In less than three years, Yvonne obtained six O levels and three A levels, and John had similar success. They married in 1971, and set up home in sheltered housing with the help and support of their parents. Determined to study further, they obtained places at the City of London Polytechnic, and also received grants. As they were both in wheelchairs, daily travel to the college was very difficult, but the Students' Union arranged fund-raising events to help cover their transport costs.

Grants

Disabled students have the same opportunity of receiving grants for further and higher education as able-bodied students. Factors such as age, level of course, parents' income, and location of home are considered. Information is contained in a brief guide, 'Grants to Students', available from the Department of Education and Science.

There are also discretionary awards paid by local education authorities, some of which are especially sympathetic towards disabled students. To obtain an adequate grant it may be necessary to approach local trusts and charities, or ex-forces associations. Some authorities are willing to give grants for special typewriters, tape recorders, or fees for readers and note-takers. If you live in Scotland, apply to the Scottish Education Department for details of such help.

74

Some local education authorities will consider making grants for students to take courses at private colleges or by correspondence.

If you are refused a grant and cannot find an alternative source of money, go back to the local authority, or to the Scottish Education Department, and ask if they can put you in touch with a charity or trust that could help. Don't be put off; persistence pays.

You can also appeal to the local Education Committee and ask the reason for their refusal to be given to you in writing. This will show you what points you could make when pursuing your appeal. It may help if you consult a councillor and ask him or her to support you.

If you are a woman, and you feel it is your sex and not your handicap that has gone against you, ask the Equal Opportunities Commission for advice: a detailed booklet is available.

If you feel that you have been refused education and training because of your racial origin and not your handicap, then approach the Commission for Racial Equality for advice.

MSC courses

The MSC pays for training and accommodation at the four residential training colleges mentioned earlier. In addition, if appropriate, trainees receive allowances for their families. These allowances are tax-free, and National Insurance contributions are credited. Full details are given in leaflet TSA L91 which is available from Jobcentres.

The MSC also provides funding for other Job Training Schemes and courses.

Benefits

Whenever your situation changes, you need to consult the DHSS about your benefit position. Make an appointment to discuss the matter fully. Ask the local office to provide you with the relevant leaflets, and study these beforehand. You can also ask the National Bureau for Handicapped Students for advice and leaflets.

Summary of education and training opportunities

- Local further education colleges

75

- University colleges and extra-mural departments
- Education colleges and institutes
- Polytechnics
- The Open University
- Access Courses (also called Higher Education Preparation Courses)
- Colleges and units run by charities and societies
- Residential 'Second Chance' colleges
- New Opportunities for Women, and similar courses
- Part-time adult education courses held in the day and evening
- Workers' Educational Association courses
- Private colleges, including secretarial and vocational
- Language schools
- Computer courses
- MSC training opportunities
- Correspondence courses
- Private tuition
- Radio and TV programmes
- Intensive short courses and seminars
- 'Teach-yourself' and similar books from libraries
- Training with employer
- Day release classes.

Conclusion

Taking a course, or studying in some way, may improve career prospects and it also has great personal value. By broadening their education and developing skills, people with disabilities can gain confidence and a greater sense of their own value, and the whole of their life can be enriched by the knowledge gained and ideas explored. Studying is also a way of making new friends.

Chapter 6

Sheltered Employment and Rehabilitation

Introduction

Many and varied schemes for sheltered employment, Community Programme employment, training and rehabilitative work that prepares for open employment, are introduced here. Provision through the MSC and voluntary bodies is described, with examples of people who have taken courses leading to a return to work or to a new career.

As a first step, people with disabilities are urged to contact a local DRO, a Specialist Careers Adviser for the Handicapped, a careers officer or a Jobcentre. Readers are reminded that leaflets setting out the training schemes in greater detail can be obtained from the centres mentioned and are urged to check the financial position for disabled people who join special schemes and programmes.

Employment Rehabilitation Centres

There are 27 such centres throughout the UK, which offer courses in industrial and commercial skills. Hospitals, GPs and Jobcentres can refer disabled people to the centres for assessment and training. Through the Job Rehabilitation Scheme, people who complete a rehabilitation course, and then take a job, are paid a special allowance for the first three weeks they spend in the new job. Courses normally last for six to eight weeks, but it is possible to stay on one for up to 26 weeks. ERC staff, as well as the careers officers, make every effort to help trainees to find a job by the end of the course.

Two of the centres, Preston and Egham, have residential units attached, while others can advise on lodgings for those who live too far away to attend daily. The centres are listed in MSC leaflet 'How your Employment Rehabilitation Centre can help you' (EPL 86).

Sue, a disabled honours graduate, has benefited from the

Preston ERC. She has been confined to a wheelchair since an operation to remove a spinal tumour left her paralysed from the waist down. Her DRO suggested she attend the residential ERC at Preston, and here she discovered that she had a flair for working with computers. With her degree in physiology and zoology, and her newly acquired computer skills, she has become the first wheelchair-bound person to work for ICI Pharmaceutical Medical Department. Apart from an additional rampway, no other modifications have been needed for Sue.

Sheltered employment

Severely disabled people, or those recovering from an illness, and finding it difficult to obtain a job in open employment, may be eligible for a place in a sheltered workshop. Such workshops are run by local authorities, voluntary organisations, Remploy, and others. At these workshops, trainees work regular hours, learn a variety of skills, and earn a basic wage, sometimes supplemented by bonus payments.

Bodies who run such workshops are continually looking for different products and new types of work that would be suitable and enjoyable for their trainees. Light engineering, pottery, gardening, furniture making, basketry, and printing are examples of the kinds of work undertaken. Many new workshops have been started under Community Programmes. For instance, at Lockwood Day Centre, Guildford, there is a School-book Renovation Project, sponsored by Community Rural Aid. This project has a high proportion of disabled workers.

The Psychiatric Rehabilitation Association has sheltered workshops for East London people who have been mentally ill. Those who attend have all been referred by social workers and doctors. These particular workshops are seen as a model for such projects, and they are often visited by others who wish to start something similar. A spokesman for the Association said to me: 'People say, "Will you come and set up a workshop like this for us?" We tell them, "No, but we will come and help you to do it".' Further information is available from the Secretary of the Groupwork Centre.

Queen Elizabeth's Foundation for the Disabled includes a large number of sheltered workshops in its *Directory of Opportunities for School-Leavers with Disabilities*. Although they are included in this directory, many of the workshops listed accept people aged 16 or 18 right up to 65.

The bodies that organise sheltered workshops include: Remploy Limited, The Spastics Society, The National Society for Epilepsy (expansion is planned so that people with other disabilities can be accepted), The Royal British Legion, Westminster Association for Mental Health, the RNIB and local societies for the blind, Camphill Village Trust, the Scottish branch of the British Red Cross, John Grooms Association for the Disabled, many local authorities, and combined efforts by local groups and voluntary societies.

Village Centres

There are some residential centres that have self-contained accommodation for disabled people, as well as factories and workshops. Perhaps the most famous of these is Papworth Everard in Cambridgeshire, the former TB Settlement, which employs 550 people, 50 per cent of whom are disabled and who between them are suffering from 81 different disabilities. The employees work in Papworth Industries making vehicle bodies, furniture for schools, travel goods, and other products. They also undertake contract engineering, electronic assembly, and mail order services.

Applications for a place in the village can be accepted from people from all parts of the UK. Enquiries should be made through Social Services Departments or the Disablement Resettlement Service (MSC).

In Hampshire, at Enham-Alamein Village Centre, there is also accommodation in family houses and hostels, and opportunities for working in cabinet making, precision engineering, bookbinding, and electronics. This village is administered in conjunction with Papworth Everard under the Village Centres Association. They aim to help those suddenly disabled by accidents, strokes, and coronaries; those suffering from deteriorating conditions; families with a severely disabled member; handicapped school-leavers; and people inappropriately housed in long-stay institutions. An initial assessment period is spent at one of the villages before acceptance. Further details can be obtained from the Secretary, Papworth Village Settlement, or from the Secretary, Enham Village Centre.

The Sheltered Placement Scheme

A DRO told me that there were many difficulties about setting

79

up sheltered workshops and finding suitable products for a mixed group of disabled people. In addition, many disabled people did not wish to spend their time solely with other disabled people in a workshop.

The MSC is now working hard to expand the Sheltered Placement Scheme which provides individual job opportunities in open employment. This scheme gives severely disabled people an opportunity to work according to their own capacity, and at their own rate, in ordinary factories, workshops and offices. The employer pays them for the amount of work produced each day, and the MSC supplements this so that the person receives a normal wage. For instance, if the disabled person is capable of 50 per cent of a fit person's output, the host firm's payment would be 50 per cent of the cost of employing a fit person to do the work. Increasingly, host firms are finding this an economical way of obtaining output and of providing employment for severely disabled people. For disabled people, it means more varied employment opportunities are available; they receive a full wage, and they work alongside able-bodied colleagues.

A number of local authorities, Remploy Limited, MENCAP, the Royal British Legion, and the Spastics Society, are among the participants in the scheme.

Under a similar MSC scheme, Sheltered Industrial Groups (SIG), disabled people work in industries in small groups, and sometimes they are paid by the local authority or a voluntary body rather than directly by the employer. Your DRO may know of local SIG schemes.

Remploy

Since 1944 Remploy has been Britain's largest employer of disabled people. The company is involved in light manufacturing and services, covering about 42 different types of businesses. These include high quality knitwear, electronic assembly, office furniture, bookbinding, surgical shoe-making, and ice cream manufacturing. There are 94 Remploy units in different parts of the country, and between them they employ over 9000 people. Pay and conditions in their workshops are agreed with trade unions, and in some places there is a pension scheme and bonus/merit scheme that boosts the rather low earnings.

People who go to work for Remploy do not necessarily have to stay. They may well wish to return to a normal working environment, having increased their skills and confidence during a period with Remploy.

With the full support of the MSC, Remploy has now launched a national programme of training within the Youth Training Scheme. Each year they hope to recruit up to 200 trainees aged from 16 to 21. The scheme will not be exclusively for disabled youngsters, as integration is seen as an important aspect of the programme, but it will help disabled young people and it is likely that some of those who join Remploy through YTS will continue as full-time employees with Remploy or in open employment. Details of the scheme can be obtained from specialist careers officers.

Rehabilitation with an existing employer

Anyone who has an accident, illness, or injury that forces him or her to be away from work for a long period should think very carefully before surrendering a job. For most people in this position it is worth making every effort to stay in an existing job. Good employers will try to keep a job open until it becomes clear whether or not the disabled person will be able to resume normal working. Keep in touch with your employer throughout the period of your recovery, and if you want to return to your job make it clear that this is your intention.

There are the following possible solutions for a person who has become disabled:

● Return to the old job
● Return to the old job with the help of aids and adaptations provided by the MSC, trade union, the National Health Service, voluntary organisations, or one's own efforts and improvisations
● Return to the old job, taking advantage of MSC schemes already mentioned
● Restructure the old job so as to remove tasks that have become too difficult
● Return to the same employer but move to a different job
● Return to the old employer on a part-time or job-share basis.

Take advantage of any convalescent opportunities given by your employer or trade union, and any rehabilitation service your company provides. Vauxhall Motors at Luton has been specially commended by the TUC for having its own rehabilitation centre to assist disabled employees to return to their normal job or to an alternative job within the company. Cadbury Limited, Keynsham, one of the winners of the 1985 'Fit for Work' awards, has for many years had an outstanding reputation for employing and retaining disabled workers. Rehabilitation is done within the firm, and jobs and hours are adjusted to suit the needs of disabled workers. Among the 79 disabled employees are amputees and people who have suffered heart conditions and nervous breakdowns. The firm says: 'The determination and motivation shown by the disabled is always noticeable.'

Community Programmes

Community Programmes offer work, full- or part-time, for up to one year on a project that is of service to the community. For a person who has become disabled and has not worked for some time, joining a community programme could be a way of returning to normality and acquiring new skill and confidence. Some of the programmes are for the benefit of disabled people. In Glasgow, an adventure playground for disabled children has been running for eight years, with funding from Urban Aid and the Scottish Adventure Playground Association. It has six Community Programme workers and three permanent staff, one of whom started as a CP worker.

In St Helens, a social worker for the deaf wanted to make sign language videos for teaching deaf people. He obtained funding from the CP Agency, advertised for workers, and found Arthur, profoundly deaf from birth, who had been made redundant from his design draughtsman job. Organisations for deaf people soon heard about the project and ordered copies of the videos on such subjects as 'Buying a House' and 'Borrowing Money'.

This is a good example of a Community Programme that has both employed and benefited disabled people.

For Chris, aged 30 and confined to a wheelchair, a CP has given him his first experience of work. He is one of 440 disabled people (10 per cent of the total number involved) currently working in County Durham Community Programmes.

Chris lives at a residential hospital for disabled people. He said recently: 'I had dreamed for years of being able to get a job, but I never had the chance before. It means so much to me just to be able to get out every day and so some real work.'

The Disablement Advisory Service arranged for a local

employment rehabilitation centre to build a ramp so that Chris can get into the workshop easily, and it helps with the cost of a taxi for his daily journey. The workshop in which wooden toys are made for local playgroups is run by the National Elfrida Rathbone Society. Chris is engaged in painting toys.

The workshop manager said: 'Disabled people obviously have special difficulties in finding jobs, but several who have worked here have gone on to permanent jobs elsewhere.' Thirty-two of the people in the workshop have physical disabilities, and 20 are educationally disadvantaged.

To find out about Community Programmes in your area, visit the Jobcentre and look at the vacancy boards. Ask your DRO or Careers Officer for advice.

You may have a link with a voluntary organisation that is heavily involved with Community Programmes. For instance, the Boys' Brigade has a slogan: 'Unemployed people working for the community on projects that would not otherwise be undertaken.' They have 20 disabled people working in their County Durham programmes, and they undertake such varied work as administration, auditing, relief for home carers, direct labour in churches, and assistance for elderly people. So find out what local societies are doing and planning in your area. Remember, as a disabled person, you will have a priority chance of a place on a Community Programme.

Financial arrangements
Work on Community Programmes is paid, but you will probably be entitled to continue receiving some of your state benefits. When you get a CP place, tell your benefit office, and they will advise you. If you earn more than a minimum amount you may have to pay National Insurance, and income tax could be deducted. So check your position carefully.

The value of part-time work
The June 1985 house bulletin of the Association of Disabled Professionals carried a statement produced by representatives of voluntary organisations on the MSC Working Group on the Quota Scheme. They recommended: 'All those who express a wish for paid employment should be given every help and facility . . . This should include those who may be in a position to work for only a few hours a week. Obstacles in the social security system to part-time employment should be removed.

Measures should be taken to encourage employment opportunities for, say, 10 or more hours a week. This will be of great help to some categories of disabled persons. The important interim function of a small number of hours' employment per week should be better recognised in the development of rehabilitation and training.' Perhaps this is something that people planning rehabilitation schemes should bear in mind.

Warning note

One DRO said to me: 'Disabled people should make sure that the Community Programme is really suitable for them; and they need to check their allowance position — they don't want to end up worse off!'

She had local people working on CPs restoring furniture and doing office work, but they were disabled in a 'very mild way'. 'Some programmes offer only two days' work a week,' she added, 'it's better to get an open job if you can. The job situation here (inner South London) is diabolical. So many jobs have just disappeared. I wish there was more we could do to help people.'

Conclusions

If you think of going on any rehabilitation programme or sheltered work experience, it is wise to visit the place before making a decision. You may think that the work would be too monotonous, or too demanding for you. On the other hand, a spell in such a setting has been a stepping stone to ordinary work for many disabled people. Be prepared to give it a try, if it seems at all suitable or hopeful. Sheltered employment can be seen as a stage in recovery — not as a destination.

A 1984 report on proposals for the development of the MSC's Rehabilitation Service said:

'The two main aims of the programme are:
  (i) To help disabled people decide which jobs are most suitable for them and what, if any, further help they need in getting those jobs
 (ii) to help disabled people to begin to return to work — the primary measure of effectiveness should be the number of clients assessed, the number that go on into jobs after further help, and the costs in each case.'

Chapter 7

Looking at Careers

Making a choice

In a letter to me, the General Secretary of the Association of Disabled Professionals said: '. . . it is harder to say what cannot be done by disabled people than what can! We have members from almost all walks of life and almost every profession. In other words, disabled people are just the same as everyone else.'

For a disabled person who is trying to choose a career, or to make a change of career, the same criteria apply as for a non-disabled person. Here are some points to consider:

- Qualifications required
- Your aptitude and skills
- Have you any experience in the field of work to which you are attracted?
- The availability of opportunities for training and entry requirements for training courses
- Employment prospects in careers that appeal to you
- Your personal interests
- Have you a strong sense of vocation to a particular type of work?
- Your own personality
- How much do you like working with other people?
- Do you want to work mainly indoors or outdoors?
- Have you a strong preference for work in town or in the country?
- Would you like to work at home?
- Is the type of work you want to do available in the area where you would like to live?
- Have you any capital or income to help you during your training and when you are qualified?
- How long are you prepared to spend in training?
- The length of time over which a career could be practised
- Have you any family links with a particular profession or trade?
- How would a particular career affect your family?

In addition, a disabled person will need to take into account the limitations imposed by his or her disability, and how far these can be overcome.

The likelihood of being able to work at home, as an employee, on a freelance basis, or in a business of your own, could also be an important factor.

Anyone trying to make a career choice would be wise to do the following homework:

- Talk to as many people as possible, asking each one about his career, how and why he chose it, the training he did, the actual work he does, the rewards, the snags and the prospects.
- Ask friends and people who know you well to suggest possible careers.
- Research widely; read books about careers; listen to programmes; watch TV and videos.
- Seek advice from careers officers, teachers, commercial careers guidance agencies, and organisations concerned with your disability.
- Study the trade and technical publications related to your career so as to ascertain job prospects and to understand the contemporary situation for people within that profession.

Remember that every career has many different specialities within it. For instance, a veterinary surgeon said to me: 'I had always intended to be a farm vet, but as things worked out, here I am working mainly with dogs.'

For anyone who has studied a language and is fluent in it, there are many possible types of work: translating, broadcasting, teaching, and in the travel industry.

People trained as nursery nurses could use their NNEB qualification for work in a hospital, day nursery, school, or as a nannie.

Often it is necessary to find the career within the career. It may be better or easier to go for good general education, or for a degree that could be used as a basis for many different careers, rather than to opt for a specialised training too soon. It all depends on how keen you are to follow a particular career, and what opportunities are available. Some people will have clearer future plans than others.

You may have been pondering your career choice for years, or you may be making a new choice because of a disability. In either case, you will want to give the whole subject of career choice a great deal of thought.

Subject areas

Accountancy
Working for a firm of accountants; as an accountant for a company, charity, or organisation; for small businesses or in private practice.
Related jobs: bookkeeping.

Administration
Openings in industry, local government, Civil Service, National Health Service (NHS), charities, insurance, commerce, and many other fields.

Advertising, public relations and market research
Those with previous experience or contacts in these fields may find openings for writing press releases or advertising copy for an agency or company.

Posts are advertised in the *Guardian* (on Mondays) and *Campaign* (weekly).

Related jobs: telephone sales of advertising space; telephone interviewing for market research.

Agriculture and horticulture
Plants, flowers, vegetables and salads could be grown and sold to retail outlets, on market stalls, to garden centres, restaurants and pubs. (See also Chapter 8.) For advice on gardening for disabled people, visit the Royal Horticultural Society demonstration gardens at Wisley.

Related jobs: The RADAR *Directory for Disabled People* suggests commercial rabbit keeping. Disability is not necessarily a bar to running a farm; in Ross-shire there is a successful farmer who is confined to a wheelchair.

Animals
Apart from veterinary surgery and veterinary nursing, there could be employment opportunities in pet shops and private kennels. In *Pet Business World*, an employer described how he engaged a totally deaf young man, without speech but with good lip reading. The trial period was a success, and the employer feels that he has found a very special employee with

patience towards animals and goodwill towards the customers. Related jobs: animal breeding, dog walking, grooming dogs and horses.

Archivist

For those with suitable qualifications, eg an arts degree, there may be openings in local museums or in stately homes where papers and books need to be catalogued or guide books produced. Companies, organisations, local government, professional bodies and church authorities sometimes require archivists to organise and catalogue their records. Museum and local history projects frequently advertise Community Programme job vacancies.

Art, craft and design

For those with gifts and skills in these fields, there are various ways of following a career, including painting pictures to sell, portraiture and quick sketches, decorating enamelware and china, patchwork, carving, lettering, pottery, making souvenirs, and offering design services, eg to printers, organisations, local companies, shops and churches. There may be scope for making and designing teaching aids for hospitals, schools, and centres for disabled people. By observation and experience, you may well know the type of material that is needed. For other ideas, see Chapter 8. Emma, who has been deaf since early childhood, is studying interior design at the London College of Furniture. She hopes to get a job designing for handicapped people.

Related jobs: art therapy, working in a gift shop, or where you can sell your products. The Design Council produces a free careers leaflet, 'Design Courses in Britain', which should help you investigate the training opportunities in your area.

Banking

Many banks employ disabled staff at all grades. Contact individual banks to discover vacancies and training programmes.

Bookbinding

This skill is often taught in sheltered workshops and adult classes. Those who become proficient could look for work with libraries and second-hand booksellers. However, it is important to consider that demand for work in this specialised field could be limited. It may be wise to find out as much as possible about prospective employers before taking a training course.

Broadcasting
People with foreign language skills could find scope in overseas broadcasting. The BBC employs disabled people in secretarial work, switchboard duties, research, producing, writing and broadcasting. Those who are keen to enter broadcasting could start by applying to local radio stations.

Careers guidance
This could be a worthwhile career for disabled people especially if they could work as DROs or Specialist Careers Officers after gaining a qualification through the Careers Service Training Council courses available. Contact the Local Government Training Board for further details.

Cartography
There are openings at O level grade and for graduates. Further information is available in the booklet 'Careers in Cartography', available from: Cartography Department, Oxford Polytechnic, Oxford OX3 0BP, and from the Civil Service Commission. James, who is completely deaf, works as a cartographer in a local government estates office.

Church work
Disability need not bar you from working for the church or any other religious establishment. Ask your parish priest, minister, or rabbi to tell you about training schemes. There are jobs in counselling, pastoral care, education, and administration.

Civil Service
There is entry to the Civil Service at different grades from age 16 to the late 50s. Publications explaining entry requirements and opportunities are available from the Civil Service Commission at Basingstoke. Vacancies are frequently advertised in local papers. There are special arrangements to assist registered disabled people who do not have the necessary educational qualifications for certain vacancies.

Computers
As there are so many openings in computers and information technology, they have been described in Chapter 9.

Drama
The 'Fair Play' campaign, launched in 1984, was established to

fight for 'equal training and employment opportunities in the arts for people with disabilities . . .' There is now more emphasis on involving disabled people in the arts, and SHAPE, established in 1976, works for greater access to the arts; it initiates workshops and provides information and advice for disabled people. There is also a growing Theatre of the Deaf. A recent report, 'Arts and Disabled People', published for Carnegie UK Trust, recommends that employers concerned with the arts should adhere to the Code of Good Practice on the Employment of Disabled People: at present, they frequently fail to fulfil their quota obligations.

Related jobs: box office work, designing and making costumes, make-up.

Fashion
Disabled people can find openings in designing and making clothes for large and small manufacturers, *haute couture*, and individual customers. There may be scope for making garments for people with special needs or unusual sizing. Marie Baker of Caldicot, Gwent, has been successful with her garments designed mainly for disabled people.

Floristry
One of the large London florists has a deaf assistant who often goes to public buildings to arrange floral displays for receptions and special occasions. There are employment opportunities with those who contract to arrange flowers in hotels, restaurants and public buildings, and florists also employ people to make wreaths and bouquets.

Invention
A disabled person who has had time to sit and think, to study objects, and sometimes to struggle with tools and appliances, may well have an idea for an invention. You may need to protect your invention by patent.

Some disabled people and parents of children with disabilities have made or adapted equipment they or their children can use. (It is claimed that the first Teddy Bear was made by Margaret Steiff who was crippled by polio — though her nephew Richard is credited with the design, invented in 1902.)

Journalism
Becoming a travel writer may seem an unlikely career for a

disabled person, but Margaret Hides follows it despite a crippling disease that makes walking very difficult. She travels world-wide, and writes for quality newspapers. There is a recognised training for journalism, conducted by the National Council for the Training of Journalists, with keen competition for places. However, some people begin by writing for magazines and local newspapers.

Local government
Most local government authorities are keen to employ disabled people. The Greater London Council (GLC) had a splendid record, and made adaptations to help disabled people, including building ramps and moving lift buttons to a convenient height. The West Midlands County Council recently received an MSC 'Fit for Work' award in recognition of their recruitment and retention of disabled workers. Ask the Personnel Department in your local town hall about job prospects, and watch advertisements in local papers.

Millinery
This is a craft in which disabled people have traditionally been employed. As well as making hats for fashion, there is also scope in re-modelling them for stage and TV productions.

Music
Performing, teaching, composing, selling musical instruments, managing groups and arranging bookings, are all possible careers for those with suitable talent. One famous British conductor is physically disabled, and there are many examples of blind musicians. Piano tuning is an established career for the visually handicapped.

Needlework
Apart from the fashion openings mentioned, keen needleworkers can find employment doing alterations and repairs for shops, dry cleaners and individuals. There is scope for knitting and selling garments, and also for designing knitting patterns for wool manufacturers.

Related jobs: embroidery, lace-making, leather-work, ecclesiastical furnishings, designing and selling in a craft, wool, or needlework shop.

Photography
There are many different spheres in which photographers have

opportunities to specialise. These include photo-journalism, portraiture, wildlife, commercial, medical, food and cookery. John Dalton has been made an Associate of the Royal Photographic Society and has won many awards for his photographs. He has been totally deaf almost since birth, but he learned to speak at a school for deaf boys.

Physiotherapy

For details of the training course for visually handicapped students, see Chapter 5.

Secretarial work

There are all kinds of openings, from office junior to chairman's secretary. With new technology, it is easier for disabled people to undertake highly skilled work. A secretarial career is one of the easiest for a disabled person to enter. Many gain promotion, and can also take a 'step sideways' into other jobs in the organisation.

Social work

People who are disabled and understand something of the needs of others could find social work a rewarding career. For information about all the different courses, contact the Central Council for Education and Training in Social Work; regional offices are listed in the telephone directory.

Speech therapy

A leaflet giving full information about this career is available from the College of Speech Therapists. This is a caring profession, suitable for people with good academic ability and a desire to help people in hospitals, clinics, assessment centres, adult training centres and schools. You need to be able to make good person-to-person contact.

Teaching

Disability could make it difficult for a qualified teacher to teach in a state school, but there may be more scope in private schools where classes can be smaller. Disabled people often lecture in colleges, polytechnics, universities and adult education. There are numerous examples of disabled teachers and lecturers who work in special schools and colleges. For example, Doncaster College has several staff who are deaf; the headmaster of Exhall Grange School, Coventry, is blind. Old buildings without lifts may make it hard for disabled people to teach in some educational institutions. If you are a qualified teacher, consider giving private tuition either in your home or in a pupil's home; if you have the necessary academic qualifications, you could try to find work marking examination papers or writing text books.

Pamela, a teacher forced by ill health to give up her job, started helping a neighbour's educationally disadvantaged child and she designed educational material for him. Now she is using her ideas to write text books and make apparatus commissioned by a publisher.

Word processing
See Chapter 9.

Writing
See Chapter 12.

Careers research

When you have studied this list, think about careers and consult books that give you more detailed information. One of the most comprehensive and authoritative is the MSC annual guide, *Occupations*, which should be available in all large public libraries. It is available from MSC, COIC Sales Department. Another concise and informative guide is *An A-Z of Careers and Jobs*, published by Kogan Page.

The MSC also produces 'Job Outlines' on particular careers, and these give details of entry requirements, training courses, and different types of work. Ask your careers officer to show you a list of the copies available. Whatever career books you consult, make sure that they are up-to-date. Training courses and addresses seem to change very rapidly, and old books may cause you to waste money on postage and telephone calls to out-of-date addresses.

Videos are another way of learning about careers. For those who wish to arrange a group showing, a free catalogue can be obtained from CFL Vision. Many of the titles are available on free loan.

Working at home

It may be easier for anyone who has restricted mobility, difficulty in using public transport, lives in a remote area, or who has commitments such as young children or elderly relatives, to pursue a career or find work to do at home. Some disabled people have little choice; if they are to follow a career or undertake any paid employment, they must find work they can do at home.

The advantages include:

- Money saved on fares or petrol
- Time and energy saved
- The person who works at home can decide when to begin and stop work, and take time off for hospital appointments, to rest, see friends or watch TV programmes; work can be done in the evening if the person wishes.
- When working at home there is not the same need to cope with other people when one feels 'down', off-colour or in pain.
- Those who work at home have more control over their working environment, including temperature, dust and noise. They can use their own toilet facilities, telephone and kitchen, which may have been adapted for their own use.

However, there are some disadvantages. These include:

- Lack of stimulation, company, conversation and competition
- No change of surroundings
- Pay is often low.

Creating the right conditions
If you work at home, make the place comfortable, conducive to work, business-like, and arranged so that the equipment you need is easily to hand.

Be disciplined. Decide when you are going to take a lunch or coffee break, and for how long. Try not to allow family or friends to interfere with your working time. Tell them that you are available in the evenings and at weekends.

Homework

Homework is traditionally poorly paid, and its availability depends on season and location. The kind of work factories put out to homeworkers includes machining, finishing, lampshade

making, cracker making, knitting, addressing and filling envelopes, and mail order. Some local authorities have an adviser whose job it is to ensure that homeworkers are not exploited. But work at home with new technology is in a very different class. Computers and word processors have opened up a whole new range of opportunities, and these will be discussed in Chapter 9.
Self-employment at home is discussed in Chapter 8.

Continuing your profession

If you are a professional person, it may be possible for you to practise your profession from your home. The sort of person who is likely to be able to do this is a solicitor, doctor, teacher, accountant, writer, journalist, hairdresser, personal counsellor, designer, layout artist, telephone salesperson, publisher's reader, or watchmaker.

Careers in industry

Within industry there are all kinds of jobs apart from work on the factory floor, at the bench, lathe, machine, loom or other equipment.

A large firm is likely to employ people in accounts, administration, catering, health and safety, management, personnel, sales, quality control, stock control, training, word processing, communications, and welfare. Even small firms will need people to undertake some of these responsibilities, though individuals may do more than one job.

Look around your local area and see what industries there are. Contact the personnel departments, and tell them what you have to offer. Perhaps they will say that they will keep you in mind when a vacancy arises, but don't leave it at that. Remind them every few months that you are available for work or could do work for them at home.

Once you get a job in a local industry, you will be able to watch out for other openings in the firm, and you will have gained experience which will stand you in good stead when you apply for advertised posts.

Be positive

When preparing for a career, or looking for a job, ability must be stressed rather than disability. If you cannot type fast and

95

accurately, you are unsuitable for a typist's job — whatever your physical condition. The important thing is that employers should select the person who can do the job well. Sometimes that person happens to be disabled but the disability is not, or should not be, the most significant thing about them. What is needed is ability. Try to convince an employer that you can do what he or she requires.

At a Barnsley factory, run by Barnsley Borough Council and part-funded by the MSC, 52 disabled people are employed producing plastic goods, from ballpoint pen tops to money boxes. The general manager said: 'There is really no difference between this factory and a normal factory. The people who work here are subject to the same rules and regulations as other people in industry. The only thing is that they are disabled, but we don't really think about it like that. I am disabled myself, because I wear glasses. It's just a matter of degree.' Machine operator Joe Speight, aged 43, described the factory as 'a godsend'. Two years ago his left hand was crushed and burned in a works accident. He was made redundant and spent 18 months on the dole. Now he is back at a machine doing an able-bodied person's work. There are no special features about his work just because he is registered as disabled: 'I am doing a normal job. This place has really put the life back into me.'

What next?

You are trained, qualified, intelligent, experienced, but you still cannot get a job or find an employer to give you work at home. You are in the same position as thousands of other unemployed people. What can you do? One big option, and a choice in which the government is prepared to give help, is self-employment. 'If no one else will employ you, employ yourself', is the MSC slogan. For ideas on starting your own business, or finding self-employment, consult the next chapter.

Chapter 8

Running Your Own Business

The pitfalls and positive help available for people considering starting their own business are outlined in this chapter. A variety of ideas for setting up a business or earning some money are offered for consideration.

The importance of assessing all the costs involved and keeping accurate accounts is emphasised. Stories of people who have started their own business — and found problems as well as success — are included.

Personal suitability for starting a business

A disabled person who wants to start a business encounters all the snags met by an able-bodied person, but in addition may suffer reduced mobility and greater fatigue, and may need to rely more on other people.

Contact with financial backers, advisers, suppliers and customers may be affected by the above factors. Nonetheless, there are disabled people among the 2¼ million or so people in the UK who are running their own businesses. Over the past five years, the average number of new businesses starting each week was 550, but in 1984 it rose to 700. Unfortunately, according to Bryan Nicholson, Chairman of the MSC, 'Too many people are still going into business without a cat in hell's chance of success.'

If you are going into business, ask yourself:

- Am I efficient at organising my own time?
- Have I done sufficient market research to see if there is a demand for my service or product?
- Can I negotiate, relate well to people, chat to customers?
- Can I reach an 'unexploited' niche of the market? Can I find a gap where demand is too low or specialised for a large company?
- Do I want to design, produce, make or sell something, from start to finish, or make it and sell it to a retailer?

- Have I thought how my business will carry on, or who could do the work, if I fall ill or need treatment?
- Have I a specialist knowledge or skill I can use in my business?
- Would it be better to do a part-time job and have a part-time business?
- Have I the energy and enthusiasm to start and follow through my scheme?
- Can I plan, finance the business, administer it, and sell the end product or service?

Obtaining help

It is worth finding out about national and local provision for people who are contemplating starting a business of their own. There are a number of government schemes, and most of these are described in the leaflet, 'How to Make your Business Grow'. To obtain a copy of this and other useful 'start-up' literature, telephone 100 and ask for Freefone Enterprise. This is the Small Firms Service, under the Department of Employment, which gives free advice to those starting small businesses.

The principal schemes include:

Enterprise Allowance Scheme

Under this scheme, people who have been unemployed for at least eight weeks can receive a weekly sum (currently £40) for a year while they are setting up in business. They are also provided with training and counselling. They must have £1000 to invest in the business themselves.

MSC courses

There are various MSC courses aimed at people wishing to set up in business. Some are intensive, and others run for up to 12 weeks. The first Graduate Enterprise Programme offered grants and training to graduates with viable ideas for starting a business. The initial course was held at Cranfield School of Management and now an additional two courses are being started in Durham and Warwick. The 36 students on the first course had plans for businesses ranging from computer software to knitware, and children's holiday camps to greetings cards.

Some courses for small businesses are run by commercial training agencies in conjunction with the MSC. Principals of small firms are allowed to attend these free of charge. Many such courses are advertised in *Executive Post*.

There are also courses designed for young people, and within the YTS there is the Genesis Programme which teaches marketing and business skills. In 1985 these courses were available in five areas of the country.

Council for Small Industries in Rural Areas (CoSIRA)

CoSIRA offers advice to those wishing to start small businesses in rural areas of England. Among those who have been helped by it are mothers of young children who have seen the need for products related to maternal and child care. Regional offices will be listed in the telephone directory.

Co-operative Development Agency

One way of starting in business is through a co-operative enterprise. There are grants and loans available for people wishing to set up in this way. Some local authorities offer their own advice and information service, and in Southwark, South London, there is a Black Enterprise Adviser. Look in local papers for information about your nearest Co-operative Development Agency, or contact the Headquarters in London.

Livewire

'A chance to work for yourself' is the slogan for this competition and advice service supported by Shell UK Ltd. It offers help to young people under 26 who want to create their own work. Everyone who enters receives encouragement and advice, and those who submit the winning ideas, projects, and action plans gain awards to help them get started. Some of the good ideas that received support in 1984-85 included a 25 year old who opened a shop specialising in selling second-hand musical instruments, and two girls who set up in business making hand-tufted rugs, after the firm where they had been making such products made them redundant. There was also the young disabled plant grower mentioned in Chapter 3.

Youth schemes

The Youth Enterprise Scheme, already mentioned in Chapter 3, provides loans of up to £3000 to help young people who want to start a business. There is also the Prince's Trust/Jubilee Trust's 'Youth Business Initiative' that offers bursaries for young unemployed people starting a business. For both these schemes you must have a well thought out plan, and only those aged 25 and under are eligible.

Buying a business

If you are keen to have your own business, it may seem easiest to buy one that is already established. But before you make any agreements or sign any documents, consider these points very carefully:

- Why is the vendor selling? Apart from any reasons he or she gives, think for yourself if there could be others.
- Beware of an over-stocked business, one that has bad debts, or a business where the person selling has worked all hours to keep afloat.
- If the vendor has been successful, remember that this may have been because of personal input. His or her good customers may not automatically support you.
- Study the accounts for the last three years.
- Consult a solicitor, an accountant, and your bank manager before commiting yourself.

It would be worth consulting *How to Buy a Business*, published by Kogan Page.

Franchising

Franchises are offered in such varied services as double-glazing, video hire, tea and coffee supplies, and catering. They are an opportunity to enter a tested business that has been successful. You pay the franchisor an initial fee and usually a percentage on all sales. Again be cautious. *Executive Post* regularly carries an advertisement warning readers that they are 'strongly advised to take professional advice before entering into any financial commitments'.

A free booklet on franchising is available from the British Franchise Association, or you could take a look at *Taking up a Franchise*, published by Kogan Page.

Business opportunity advertisements

These advertisements proliferate in some newspapers and magazines. Approach these 'opportunities' with great caution. They may not be as 'easy' as they seem. If the literature is cheap or free, it may be worth sending for some, not necessarily to take up the scheme advertised, but to spark off your own ideas. Before parting with any money, ask a consumer association for advice. Be suspicious if replies are to be directed to a box number.

Premises

It is often cheaper to work from home when starting up, but before you do so, check the terms of your lease to find out if it is permissible to run a business from your house or flat.

If you decide to rent business premises, research their suitability for your purpose, and check with your local planning officer and fire department in case any work needs to be carried out before you start trading. Consult a solicitor before signing the lease or putting up any money. Further information is given in *How to Choose Business Premises*, published by Kogan Page.

Finance

When starting a business, you need to know how to keep simple accounts. If necessary, buy or borrow a book to teach yourself. Perhaps you have a friend who could advise you?

You must be able to chart your actual weekly or monthly sales — it helps if you can make a bar chart or graph so that you can see your position at a glance. You need a target break-even figure which is the value of sales you need to make before you go into profit. If you are not achieving sufficient sales, the business will not be profitable.

When calculating your break-even figure, you need to allow for overheads such as rent, rates, lighting, heating, insurances, postage, telephone, stationery (or for extra heating and lighting costs if you are at home all day). There may be expenses for petrol or taxis, as well as for materials or stock. If your turnover is sufficiently high (£20,500 a year in 1986-87), you will also have to make provision for Value Added Tax.

Those who employ people have to earn enough to pay the salaries and National Insurance contributions, and allow for sick pay and holidays. When you start your business it may well be a one-man band, but even so it would be wise to allow sufficient money to pay for emergency help. You also need to bear in mind the risk of bad debts, which have ruined many a small business.

It may be necessary to employ someone to help you with the accounts and prepare your tax returns for the Inland Revenue.

When you have done all your homework and research you may realise that the prospects for your business are very uncertain. At this stage it may be wise to abandon the idea, or at least postpone starting your business, rather than rushing ahead and losing your capital or any compensation money you may have received. There is government money available for helping people start businesses. To qualify for this you need to produce a viable proposal.

Banks and insurance companies are well aware of the risks run by those starting a small business, and they try to give guidance and information. You could send for the National Westminster Bank's free 'start-up' literature from your local branch. The Midland Bank has four booklets and a video with their 'Build a Successful Business' material. The Legal and General Insurance Company produces 'The Self-Employed Report', available free.

If you have a bank account, your branch can be very helpful. When you start a business, you will probably need an account.

Business structure

You can work as a sole trader, in a partnership, or as a limited company.

A sole trader owns the business and is responsible for all the decisions, takes all the profits, and is responsible for all the debts; if he or she becomes bankrupt, the sole trader's personal assets can be seized to satisfy creditors. He or she can employ others and trade under his or her own name or another. Sole traders pay class 2 National Insurance contributions and, when annual profits exceed £4450, class 4 as well, which is 6.3 per cent. Some businesses start off as sole traders, then develop into partnerships or limited companies.

A partnership is jointly owned by one or more people, but is otherwise similar to a sole trader. It is advisable to have a partnership agreement drawn up by a solicitor spelling out the terms of formation, dissolution and division of profits and responsibilities, even when only husband and wife are involved. Never go into partnership with people you know nothing about; you will be responsible for any debts they run up on behalf of the business even though you were unaware of what was happening.

A limited company has two or more shareholders, one of whom must be a director. A company secretary is also required, and your solicitor or accountant might act in this capacity. You will need a solicitor to set up the company in the first place and register it. Specific accounting requirements are laid down in the Companies Acts, and the audited accounts must be submitted annually to the Registrar of Companies. The directors' financial liability is limited to the face value of their shares, unless they have given personal guarantees to the bank to raise loans. Taxation on companies is different from that charged on sole traders and partnerships.

Marketing your business

As a small business, you may be able to offer these features that a large company cannot provide:

- Speed of response to orders
- Keen prices based on low overheads
- Friendly personal service
- High quality products
- Willingness to supply small quantities.

However good your service or product, you must make it known to get enough sales. Consider these publicity methods:

- Advertisement or news item in church magazines
- Publicity in local papers — you could offer to be interviewed and photographed for a feature
- News items on local radio
- Advertisements on newsagents' boards and on free supermarket boards
- Small poster on public library notice board, in clinics, surgeries, day centres and community centres (if they permit commercial notices)
- Letter or card sent to local organisations, parent-teacher groups, local history societies, senior citizens' clubs, as appropriate
- Word of mouth through friends.

Success story

One disabled person who has started his own business is Dave who has been confined to a wheelchair since a swimming accident 20 years ago. He is unable to walk, and has only part use of his hands and arms. However, his technical skills and enthusiasm to become self-employed so impressed the MSC that he was awarded a grant to set up and equip a hi-tech workshop in a former shed at the Cheshire Home in Lancashire where he lives.

'One of the best moments of my life was the morning I woke up and it was the first day of my having my own business,' said Dave. Before setting up his company Dave did his own market research. In his workshop he repairs radio cassettes, music centres, calculators, portable TVs, and similar equipment sent to him by local firms. Before the accident, Dave had completed six months as an apprentice in an electrical shop, and he has also taught himself watch and clock repairs. After he was disabled, he took a two-year electrical engineering course, and passed with honours.

This is thought to be the first time that a resident of a Cheshire Home has become self-employed while being a resident. A spokesman for the Foundation said that, as a result of Dave's success, they plan to examine ways in which more of their residents could benefit from MSC help.

Dave is a very exceptional person, and he was fortunate in having a skill on which he could build after becoming disabled.

Self-employment at home

All the above information may seem hopelessly irrelevant and unrealistic for you. Only a small percentage of people are able to run a small business successfully. Legal and General Insurance estimate that statistically the average self-employed person works a 55-hour week and has 16 days' holiday a year. You may well feel that you could not possibly put in this time and effort. Conditions vary in different parts of the country, and the project that works in one place may not be successful elsewhere. The degree of mobility, experience and strength of character is as individual among disabled people as among the rest of the population.

However, although you may feel that you could not possibly run a business, you may well have a skill, hobby or interest that you could use to earn some money from home.

Here are some ideas to consider:

- Growing or making a product to sell
- Dealing in a specialised commodity, eg local history books
- Offering a service, eg mending, ironing, gardening

- Running a hire service, eg maternity wear, theatrical costumes
- Giving private lessons or coaching
- Undertaking secretarial work, typing and word processing
- Telephone answering service for small businesses
- Running a mail order service.

Hobbies that could be used to earn money

- Gardening
- Breeding tropical fish and growing plants for aquaria
- Pottery
- Cookery — cakes, catering for parties and special occasions
- Bees and honey
- Jigsaws — running a library
- Needlework — repairs, alterations, dressmaking, button and belt covering, smocking, designing tapestry kits, and making commemorative samplers
- Embroidery — eg motifs for a team
- Upholstery and curtain making or altering
- Knitting — Fair Isle and Guernsey sweaters, and finishing-off service
- Designing and hand-printing labels and cards for shops and businesses
- Photography
- Caring for pets
- China repairs
- Making and mending dolls and toys
- Writing — see section in Chapter 12
- Giving talks or lectures on your hobby or special interest to groups, such as Women's Institutes, for a fee. Those who are expert in their field may be able to arrange to give a course of lectures through the Workers' Educational Association or at local education centres.

If you study books on the subject of your hobby and earning at home, and think about it, you will probably come up with plenty of other ideas.

Unusual enterprise
'Anything Nostalgic' is the name that Pam and Bill chose for their finding and research service. It began when Pam, frustrated by the difficulties of obtaining employment, decided to set up her own business.

Blindness had not prevented both Pam and Bill from gaining Open University degrees and BA Honours from Reading University, but despite these academic qualifications both found it difficult to obtain suitable jobs.

'Blow them, I'll be my own boss,' decided Pam. Bill found a teaching job, but later he gave it up to help Pam with the business.

They locate books, articles, photographic props, and unusual items; quote the price to the enquirer; and obtain them if the enquirer wishes to proceed. They have many contacts and keep well organised braille records but, even so, it seems remarkable that they are able to run such a business. They welcome enquiries to Anything Nostalgic, 35 Northcourt Avenue, Reading RG2 7HE; 0734 871479.

Hard work and hopes

'What I wanted was to be my own boss and to work out of doors, preferably growing things,' explained Clive. He walks with the aid of two sticks, but at the herb nursery he and his able-bodied wife have started, he manages to do most jobs except the lifting and carrying of heavy objects.

Clive and his wife grow about 200 different herbs, and sell them at markets and shows and by post. Despite long hours of hard work, they have not made a profit so far, and if they do not manage to do so this summer they will be forced to reconsider their position. However, they are hopeful and full of ideas for developing the business.

If you would like a copy of their herb catalogue, write (enclosing sae) to Coombe Herbs, 1 Beaumont Cottages, Gittisham, Nr Honiton, Devon EX14 0AG.

Making money from your home

Readers who are owner-occupiers may have spare rooms they could let profitably. But be cautious. Once you have let a room it can be hard to regain possession, even if the tenant is unsatisfactory. Study the free guide, 'Letting rooms in your house', available from the Citizens' Advice Bureaux or the Department of the Environment.

The DHSS will advise you how rent received will affect your benefits. Remember that income from letting is taxable, so think carefully. If you are no better off as a result, it is not worth the worry of having someone else living in your home.

If you decide to let a room, it is probably wisest to approach a local college and ask if they need short-term accommodation for students. Or perhaps a guest house would be glad to send you occasional overflow guests. As a disabled person with restricted hearing, mobility or vision, you will be vulnerable, so beware of taking the wrong tenant into your home. With the right person living or staying in your home, you could gain companionship as well as additional income.

Further information and advice

A number of titles containing business ideas have been published by Kogan Page, and these are listed in Chapter 15. It is worth spending plenty of time reading before starting your business. Look for these and other titles in a bookshop or public library.

'Signposts to Self-Employment', a new information pack from Project Full-Employ, is available from the Self-Employment Resource Centre.

Conclusion

Starting one's own business is an attractive idea but there are many factors to consider before embarking on such a project. It is vital to think carefully, seek reliable advice and consider prospects realistically.

Chapter 9

Information Technology (IT)

Introduction

Information technology and modern computer systems have transformed life for many people. The technology can be applied to daily living and also to the work carried out by people with disabilities. For instance, Optacon enables blind people, working in a variety of spheres, to read printed text, while 'talking word processors' are used by blind people already following a career — eg visually handicapped physiotherapists who keep records with the aid of such equipment.

The new technology has also created new jobs, such as word processing, that disabled people can do. On the other hand, it must be mentioned that IT has also caused the loss of jobs traditionally performed by disabled people.

Equipment such as teletext, visual display units, word processors, remote work units, computer-based learning and training centres, microcomputer controlled toys for handicapped children, portable terminals such as Vistel which send printed conversations across the lines, and electronic mail systems such as Prestel Mailbox, have brought new freedom, independence and confidence to thousands.

Computers are a fast growing area of employment with opportunities for all kinds of skills. They are used in a great variety of industries — insurance companies, banks, finance companies, engineering and manufacturing industries, public administration and defence, retail, transport and construction companies, travel and estate agencies, and libraries are all among the users.

There has been a drive to make sure that every school has at least one computer, but this seems scarcely adequate. Professor Tom Stonier, of the Department of Science and Society at the University of Bradford, pleaded for a computer 'for every child', when he addressed the Institute of Directors recently. He said that such provision with a computer system to be used at home and at school would ensure that 'the country became truly at home with computers . . . It would stimulate the economy and create the kind of intellectual infrastructure to assure a technologically literate society in the next century.'

If the aim is to be 'one computer per child', perhaps the nation could start by providing one for every disabled child or young person who could possibly use it. New technology can be used as eyes, ears, hands and voice for a disabled child or adult. If you are a disabled person, or the parent of a disabled child, find out all you can about the computers that are available. A recent, useful book is *Computer Help for the Disabled* by L Ridgway and S McKears, published by Souvenir Press.

Information on special educational needs now appears on Prestel — it is called Special Educational Needs Database (SEND), and although originally set up for users in Scotland, much of the information is of interest to viewers elsewhere in the UK.

By learning to use a word processor, computer, or other IT equipment, people who have had to abandon a previous career after accident or injury can learn a new trade or profession and do jobs using IT equipment. Such computer-based systems, teaching computing and word processing, have been so popular when introduced at Stoke Mandeville Hospital that 50 per cent of patients leaving have bought their own computers.

The Head-Start work station, conceived and developed at the National Spinal Injuries Unit, Stoke Mandeville, makes it possible for even the most severely disabled people to use more than 1000 unmodified computer programs unaided. These programs will enable the users to write, draw and compose music; they can be used for employment, entertainment or studying.

Three of these work stations are now in use at Stoke Mandeville. Each has been designed for individuals to use with whatever movements they can perform. The work stations cost upwards of £3500 which includes the computer, printer and a selection of games and other programs.

Case study

Recently I received this letter:

'With reference to your request for career information, I thought that you might be interested in my own experiences. I am 39 years old, and was born in Warrington. I contracted

polio at 11 months old, which left me fairly severely disabled.
I am, however, reasonably mobile with the aid of a full-
length calliper and a stick; also I own and drive an automatic
car.

'I was educated at a normal secondary modern school,
and left at the age of 15 without any qualifications. (My
childhood was punctuated by long stays in hospital which
left great gaps in my education, making it difficult to pass
exams.)

'On leaving school I managed to secure a place at the
Queen Elizabeth Training College for the Disabled to train
as a draughtsman. This was, I am afraid, doomed to failure
as I did not have the mathematical skills required. I was,
therefore, transferred to a bookkeeping course which I
successfully completed.

'I left the college in 1963 and gained employment as a
junior in the accounts department of a television rental
company. I stayed there for two years until, in 1965, I
switched to the local Ford main agency as a clerk.

'I was made redundant from the Ford main agency in
1968, and three months later joined the staff at the Premium
Savings Bond office as a clerical assistant.

'I wasn't really suited to the Civil Service atmosphere at
Premium Bonds, so found another job as quickly as I could.
This was with British Aerospace as a clerical/admin officer
in the spring of 1969.

'I have been with British Aerospace ever since. I have,
however, had problems as far as gaining promotion is
concerned. I put this down to the fact that I was an ill-
educated clerk in a technical area. I worked in the
mathematical services departments which programs and
runs the computer.

'About three years ago I saw a notice asking for volunteers
to train as computer programmers. I applied, and much to
my surprise passed the stringent aptitude test. I was then
transferred to the training school for two years' training.
I am now back in my old office as a fully fledged computer
analyst programmer.

'I always felt that I was under-utilised in my previous job,
but couldn't see any way round it unless I could get further,
specific training. This is, of course, easier said than done.
I didn't even know what I would be capable of or good at,
and it's difficult to take on intensive study while holding

110

down a full-time job.

'I guess that at the end of the day I have a lot to be thankful to British Aerospace for. I now have a demanding, interesting job, which leaves me feeling a fulfilled and useful member of society.'

Remote working

As well as the more obvious computer related work, such as programming, record keeping and word processing, today's technology enables many other tasks to be carried out effectively in the home. These include estimating, stock control, and bookkeeping.

Employers often find that overheads are reduced when they do not have to provide working space for employees, and also that employees are more efficient when working at home away from distractions and without the inconvenience of commuting. In addition, a disabled person working at home is often highly motivated and productive.

In a few years' time homeworking may become a way of life for many more of the population. In the past, work at home has often been boring, undemanding, and poorly paid. Now, with remote work units, there are more opportunities for good jobs with flexible working hours for able-bodied and disabled people who wish to work at home.

Those suffering from a wide range of disabilities, including multiple sclerosis, spina bifida, the effects of polio, rheumatoid arthritis, progressive muscular atrophy, brittle bone disease, haemophilia, and paralysis following accidents, have all proved they can undertake the work successfully. They took part in pilot schemes introduced by the Department of Trade and Industry (DTI), and are now doing stimulating and satisfying work that diminishes the effects of their disability and emphasises their ability.

To promote the use of IT by disabled people, the DTI set up the first pilot project with six disabled people in remote work units. This experiment was so successful that the scheme was extended and a further 58 disabled people were given remote work units. The jobs involved had to be worthwhile and provide at least 20 hours' employment per week, with pay in line with salaries received by able-bodied people doing similar jobs.

More units are now being set up, and lessons learned from the pilot scheme have been incorporated in the project. Phase 2 which ran until August 1986 and set up a further 50 home-based jobs.

The project aims to establish guidelines that will help the MSC if they should decide to make this kind of provision for people with disabilities. The pilot project is organised by IT World Ltd.

DROs and the Disablement Advisory Service are being encouraged to tell companies about the benefits of remote work units, and to check if disabled people have skills, enthusiasm, and home circumstances that would make them suitable for the project. If the idea of working on a remote work unit appeals to you, discuss it with your DRO.

Individuals who have taken part in the pilot schemes include Graham, who monitors and evaluates educational computer software and prepares programs for the National Star Centre; Richard, who keeps the stock control records for two public houses in Northern Ireland; Kenny, who provides a central computer software resource for schools throughout the Western Isles; Rodney, a self-employed accountant, who undertakes work for local firms in Hertfordshire; and Frances, who does word processing for reference books and course material used by the London School of Accountancy.

One very exceptional person, a 17 year old boy, who is only two feet tall, has brittle bone disease, and is limited to a reclining position in a wheelchair, works on a keyboard installed in his home. He feeds information into a Health Board computer and retrieves data from it for local Health Board staff in the Western Isles of Scotland where he lives. This young man, who has been a computer fan from an early age, is an avid learner, very bright, and keen to have as full a life as possible. His training for this job was organised through the Industrial Training Throughout With an Employer (ITTWE) scheme. The Western Isles Health Board who employ him has been so impressed by his progress and with the feasibility of the scheme, that it has obtained a Scottish Office grant to set up remote terminals for staff on other islands.

New Outlook (an MSC publication) also gives examples of people who have found careers using new technology.

Visually handicapped people and IT

One of the traditional occupations for visually handicapped people has been audio-typing, but word processing, which

112

relies on using a screen, has put some of this employment at risk. However, the RNIB has set up a training programme so that blind people can learn to use word processors with a voice output, enlarged visual display units, or Versa braille units that enable texts to be checked and edited in braille.

The RNIB word processing training takes very small numbers as it is meant to demonstrate what is possible — it is not a general training programme. The Institute's Vocational Research Officer said: 'What we hope to show is how employers can do this training themselves.' Further information on the project, details of the methods and equipment that can be used by blind people, and examples of visually handicapped people who are working with computers, are contained in the RNIB's booklet, 'Working with Computers'.

Another example of IT being used by visually handicapped people involves blind physiotherapists (there are over 500 in the UK). Since 1984 several of them have been using a work station supplied by the MSC. These work stations accept braille and text input that can be translated, edited, stored and printed with the aid of a spoken output. They are used to store and update patients' records and for general communication.

Disablement Advisory Service

The DAS are 'problem solvers' as well as providers of equipment, loans, and grants for adaptations. Equipment for visually handicapped and disabled people is being improved constantly, and the DAS tries to keep up to date with developments. It gives advice on such items as keyboard and visual display units linked with ordinary telephones for deaf people, office furniture, and 'scooter' type wheelchairs for faster movement within an office complex. There is also a LEVO chair for people in wheelchairs who need to reach high shelves.

The assessment courses run by the MSC assess and retrain individuals and advise employers how such people could best carry out their work.

Some hospitals have specialist medical rehabilitation centres that work with the patient and the employer when someone has been seriously ill, perhaps with a heart attack, and modifications are needed so that the person's old job can be retained.

Through units such as these, through new technology, and with help from the MSC, DTI, and other bodies, work opportunities for some disabled people are expanding.

Gerry, a draughtsman who developed multiple sclerosis, was finding it difficult to travel to work, but the DTI provided his employer with a grant towards the cost of computer equipment, and the MSC provided the training and tutors from the local IT centre, so that now Gerry can work at home on computer programs for his employer. 'This is completely different from any work that I have done before. Re-training has saved my career. I am sure there are plenty of other disabled people who could do what I have done, and I hope others will take advantage of the help which is available.'

As well as providing new opportunities for employment at home, computers have made a tremendous difference to the quality of life for severely disabled people. The *Sunday Times'* 'A Life in the Day of . . .' recently featured Ann Armstrong, paralysed by polio, who has spent 30 years on a respirator. With her toe she is able to push a button on a panel and control her television, radio, lighting, and computer. In 1963 she founded the magazine *Responaut* for disabled people, their families, engineers and medical staff, and she still edits it. When talking about her life, she said: 'I plan to spend the next 25 years tapping out books on my computer by sending it morse instructions with my toe.'

At a Cheshire Home in Kent, some residents are too severely disabled to communicate at length by speech, or to put pen to paper, but with microcomputers they can communicate and 'chat' with other residents as well as writing letters to family and friends, and deal with their own business correspondence. Other residents use microcomputers for learning.

This is an exciting Community Programme project, using unemployed graduates who have an interest in computing but insufficient experience to gain a job with computers. They spend time helping each resident learn how to use the equipment; one resident uses a stick held in her mouth, and others operate the equipment by foot, fist, chin or cheek. Many visitors come to see this project, and the residents enjoy demonstrating their skills.

Inventions and adaptations to enable more people to use computers are being developed constantly. A new 'hands-free' method is based on an American device with a headset that translates head movements into cursor movements. The potential for using the unit to help the disabled was spotted by the managing director of a Liverpool computer agency who had become familiar with the problems of the handicapped after a relative had been disabled in a car crash. Previous devices to enable severely disabled people to operate computers often depended upon cumbersome mechanical links to a keyboard, but the 'hands-free' method is much simpler.

Such projects and experiments are being carried out all over the country, and computer aids are giving new opportunities to disabled children, young people and adults. There is enormous potential in this area. When a person has lost the power of speech, for instance, after an operation for cancer, think what it could mean if a computer and screen were available through which he or she could 'converse' with medical and nursing staff as well as friends, relations and fellow patients.

Finding software for your needs

The Disabled Living Foundation, Production Engineering Research Association and the Newcastle upon Tyne Polytechnic Handicapped Persons Research Unit have all received funding from the Department of Trade and Industry towards the development of databases (on computers) for the storage and retrieval of information on the needs of disabled people.

At Newcastle upon Tyne Polytechnic, the Handicapped Persons Research Unit has prepared a database (Bardsoft) containing information on a wide range of computer software that would be of help to people with special needs. If you have a query that could be answered through the Bardsoft database, write to the Unit and tell them what sort of program you require. They can search under headings such as communication, assessment, teaching, employment and recreation. Enclose an sae and 10p per subject search fee.

The HPRU also has a database concerned with non-medical research for the disabled.

Computer training

For anyone keen to obtain a job or find a better job, computer training can open the door. Jobs in computing include: selling hardware (mainly the computers and peripheral equipment), selling software (the programs), data preparation, data control, computer operating and programming, and systems analysis.

Courses are offered at all levels, from Open Entry courses which do not require any particular academic qualification, to

115

postgraduate courses. For instance, in Lambeth there are short introductory courses one evening each week for eight weeks, one day a week courses, and full-time courses. There are YTS computer courses, and also MSC courses for students of 19 or over, educated to A level standard. These include computer programming, information processing and data. Some residential colleges, such as Queen Elizabeth's, include computer programming in courses. There is also MSC Wider Opportunities Training that teaches computer use. To find out more about any of these opportunities, contact your DRO or Specialist Careers Adviser. You can also obtain information by writing to the National Computing Centre, Oxford Road, Manchester M1 7ED. Some of the colleges and bodies mentioned in Chapter 5 will also have information about courses.

There are a great many computer magazines, and you may like to browse through these in a library to see if they would be useful for you.

Setting up on your own with a word processor

Having become skilled on a word processor, you may think of starting up a service doing work for local companies or professional people. Your first problem will be purchasing the word processor. You need good advice about this, as there is such a variety available. Study those used at the centre where you learned computer skills; attend a business equipment exhibition if this is possible; study newspaper articles and advertisements; be willing to take advice from every quarter, and search around to find the right equipment for your particular purpose.

Recently, a journalist writing in *The Times* described the problems she had experienced because she sent her husband to buy a word processor for her. She found the instruction book complicated and difficult to understand, and she felt that the machine she ended up with was not necessarily the best choice for her. However, she would not be without the word processor. 'For a writer who re-writes and edits as much as I do it has been a boon.' She feels that her introduction to it could have been easier, and she could still do with advice that she doesn't know how to find. Her experience emphasises the importance of buying wisely and of having a thorough training in how to use your computer.

If you work at home with a word processor, do not be

tempted to spend long, continuous hours at the screen as this is a strain on the eye muscles. Make sure you have your screen suitably positioned for lighting — no glare should be allowed. Ideally, the lamp should shine on your script and not on your screen. You need to rest your eyes periodically by looking into the distance and where it is relatively dark. A 10-minute break in each hour is advisable. Some people find that sitting at a word processor makes their neck and shoulders stiff, and it can be tiring, so do not be a slave to your machine.

Practical Action

This body helps charities obtain the equipment they need for efficient working. Computers and word processors are sometimes available free or at low cost when companies update their hardware and give their old equipment to charity. If you belong to a group that could benefit under this scheme, contact Practical Action.

Note to parents

Some handicapped children and young people have opportunities to learn to use computers in special or ordinary schools. Encourage your child to take every such chance that is offered. If skill in information technology can be acquired, his or her communication abilities will be vastly improved and life in general made more normal.

Simple boards enabling children to press buttons and spell out messages, or read messages rapidly, and take part in meetings or conversations, give handicapped youngsters more control over their lives. A boy in a wheelchair with a pocket board on his lap can easily ask for what he wants, or say where he wants to go, even if he cannot speak. Being able to communicate with other people is an essential human attribute that can be taken for granted.

An Optacon screen enables blind people to read ordinary print, and another form of display screen magnifies small type for people with limited sight. There are many new technological aids being developed all the time. These aids and computers give people a new enthusiasm for living, closer contact with other people, and a sense of achievement. See that your child obtains maximum benefit from all this new, exciting technology.

One of the important developments for children has been the government's Microelectronics Education Programme (MEP). This included provision for children with special educational needs. Four centres (Bristol, Manchester, Redbridge and Newcastle) were set up to encourage and help schools and teachers introduce IT into schools for children with special needs.

Though the Microelectronics Education Programme ended in April 1986, the Special Education Section of the programme has been promised support for another three years.

In addition, with their 'IT and the Disabled' scheme, the Department of Trade and Industry has set up numerous projects in schools and colleges.

As Mr Kenneth Baker MP said, when addressing the British Association for the Advancement of Science, 'Information technology is a flexible and versatile technology . . . it has a vast potential to make our lives fuller, less bound by formality and the need to move physically from one place to another. These are benefits we will all come to appreciatt but, I believe, they will make a truly significant difference for the disabled and increase their chances of playing a more active role in society.'

Chapter 10

Equipment for Living

The right equipment can make an enormous difference to life when you are disabled. I know that the so-called 'cosmetic calliper' from the Royal National Orthopaedic Hospital at Stanmore has made walking easier and less tiring for my husband. For over 25 years he wore a full-length, old-fashioned, steel and leather calliper which often broke, sometimes caused painful sores, and necessitated manual locking and unlocking every time he sat down or stood up. A cosmetic calliper is made partly from moulded plastic and is worn inside the shoe (which may need to be built up and bought half a size larger than for the old-fashioned type of calliper which has a metal frame fastened to the outside of the shoe heel.) A cosmetic calliper is far lighter, more comfortable and less conspicuous than the traditional version.

It was only through listening to the BBC programme 'Does he take Sugar?' that we heard about these modern callipers. They were not available at our local hospital, but fortunately my husband had been a patient at Stanmore when he was recovering from polio many years before, and they agreed to see him and make one for him.

Now, whenever we meet anyone who wears the old type of calliper, we tell them about this new one. It is surprising how many disabled people and professionals in the field have never seen one. The message is, look around for yourself, ask, listen, visit showrooms if you can, and study publications for disabled people. Don't automatically rely on other people to tell you what is available.

Disabled Living Foundation

The Foundation has an information service which aims to collect and keep up-to-date information concerning all aspects of daily living for disabled people. It answers telephone and letter enquiries from disabled people, their families and friends, and has a large showroom displaying aids and adaptations. These include the BBC Radio 'In touch' kitchen, clothing, wheelchairs, hoists, and recreational aids such as musical instruments. In addition, there is an area where video and tape slides on aids and equipment can be studied. The reference library, with its comprehensive stock of books, leaflets and journals, can be visited (by appointment) and the librarian will supply reading lists.

The Foundation produces a range of publications on all aspects of disabled living, and these are constantly being updated. Subjects covered include Housing and Design of Furniture, Incontinence, Visual Handicap, Music, and Physical Recreation. Write to the Foundation for a current list and order form. Aids are not on sale at the centre but advice is given on costs and where to purchase equipment. Telephone enquiries can be made Monday to Friday from 9.30 am to 5.00 pm, on 01-239 6111.

The Foundation can supply a list of other aid centres throughout the UK. Some of these are run by commercial organisations and others by voluntary bodies. The Scottish Council on Disability has a travelling exhibition. For further information about this, contact the Council in Edinburgh. Wales Council for the Disabled at Caerphilly has a small exhibition centre. There are also centres in Manchester, Birmingham, Belfast, Merseyside, Newcastle upon Tyne and elsewhere. Your local council or association for the disabled should be able to suggest the nearest place where you can visit an exhibition.

Boots the Chemist sells a range of aids for disabled people, and these can be inspected in larger stores. A catalogue is available at most branches.

Commercially produced aids and adaptations
Magazines produced for disabled people, for social workers and those working with disabled people, and publications produced by disability organisations, frequently carry advertising for all kinds of equipment, including chair lifts, sanitary fixtures, incontinence aids, wheelchair accessories, clothing, trolleys and go-carts for children. If you are thinking of buying any of these, first seek advice from a body such as RADAR or the Disabled Living Foundation, from physiotherapists or any centre where you are receiving treatment. Perhaps you will be able to see the equipment being used in a hospital or residential home, or you will know someone else who has purchased it.

No one wants to waste money on equipment that is going to be disappointing or unsuitable.

The Royal Association for Disability and Rehabilitation

RADAR aims to help disabled people lead full and useful lives. This help includes giving advice on education, welfare and housing. RADAR advises designers, local authorities, and commercial organisations on access for disabled people. Its publications give details of new mobility aids and appliances. Individuals can be given advice on their entitlement to local authority services and state provision.

Provision of aids and appliances

Aids for medical and nursing care at home can be supplied through the National Health Service, if prescribed by a doctor. Body appliances are usually obtained on the recommendation of a hospital consultant. Artificial limbs are supplied and maintained under the NHS. Many other items can be obtained through the DHSS.

Sometimes an aid is wanted but there is no NHS or DHSS provision for it. Under these circumstances, a disability society or a local charity may be willing to make a grant. Help with buying electric wheelchairs is often given in this way. When an aid is needed by an individual, particularly a child, local organisations may be willing to hold a sponsored event or some other money raising effort. Memorial funds also help in such cases. A family that has lost a child may well prefer that money should be given for equipment for a handicapped child rather than being spent on funeral flowers.

Cooking and household organisation

British Gas tries to make life easier for disabled people. It produces a range of adaptations and special controls, and will gladly send a Home Service Adviser to your home to give advice. There is no charge for this service. For further information and leaflets, contact your nearest Gas Board.

The Electricity Council has a leaflet, 'Making life easier for Disabled People', which describes attachments for switches and appliances. Copies of the leaflet are available in Electricity Board showrooms.

A pack of design sheets on aspects of house design for disabled people has been published by the Centre on Environment for the Handicapped. This pack is aimed at architects and housing officers, but it would be useful for anyone who is having a house or bungalow built for them.

Aids for the visually handicapped

The Royal National Institute for the Blind (RNIB) markets a great many different items especially designed for visually handicapped people. These include clocks, watches, embossed maps, and games that are planned so that visually handicapped and sighted people can play them together. The RNIB provides all kinds of advice and help for visually handicapped people, and it has done a great deal to promote the use of modern technology and to train blind people so that they can make good use of it for leisure and employment. Contact the RNIB if there are any problems you wish to discuss concerning educational provision, training, aids, employment, and holiday accommodation.

The famous British Talking Book Service is open to any visually handicapped people who can provide a certificate to show that they have defective reading vision.

There are numerous other organisations and clubs that provide tapes and recordings for visually handicapped people. These are listed in the RADAR *Directory*. One of particular interest is the National Newspaper and Magazine Tape Service for the Blind that produces cassette versions of local weekly newspapers for distribution to visually and physically disabled people. Details can be obtained from the Service.

Services for deaf people

The Royal National Institute for the Deaf (RNID) is concerned that 'all deaf and hard of hearing people shall be full menbers of the community'. It has a freely available professional technical service for deaf people, and this handles some 20,000 enquiries each year. Advice is provided on all aspects of hearing, hearing impairment, and aids. The development of new devices is a major part of the technical department's work, and it is constantly seeking to open up new avenues by which deaf people may enter into personal communication with others. The best way of keeping in touch with the Institute's work seems to be through their magazine, *Soundbarrier*. This is full of information, personal stories, reviews of new books and equipment, readers' letters, and in-depth articles. Anyone who is deaf, or who has a member of their family with hearing impairment, would profit greatly from reading this magazine. A comprehensive list of the RNID publications, and information about its work can be obtained from the Institute.

The Royal Association in Aid of the Deaf and the Dumb (RADD) has trained staff who act as interpreters, give practical advice on everyday problems, arrange social events and church services for deaf/blind and deaf people who live in their own homes or in institutions. If you would like a visit, or help with transport to a meeting or service, contact RADD.

Help with speech and language problems

The College of Speech Therapists publishes a number of useful leaflets, including 'Without Words', for the relatives of a stroke patient.

The Association for All Speech Impaired Children (AFASIC) is very strong on support for parents, and is a source of encouragement and advice to those whose children have speech disorders. Their book list is available by post.

Occupational aids

Until recently there has been no central service offering information and advice on occupational aids and adaptations. Now, with help from the European Social Fund, the MSC, and the Department of Trade and Industry, a pilot project has been started to demonstrate the importance of having an information and advisory service on occupational aids, and how they can contribute to the more effective employment of disabled people.

The pilot service is being carried out by the Production Engineering Research Association (PERA). People who use aids in their work, or who have had equipment adapted to help them to do a job, are asked to tell PERA about their aids so that they can assemble as much information as possible. Please telephone the project leader on 0664 64133 Ext 362, or write to PERA, if you have an experience to contribute or would like advice.

Rehabilitation Engineering Movement Advisory Panels (REMAP)

This voluntary organisation is part of RADAR, and it has about 90 groups in different parts of the UK. They are formed by local doctors, social workers, teachers, engineers, craftsmen, and representatives of disability organisations. The panels are concerned with solving problems of mobility, daily living and occupational work, and they modify, adapt or invent aids to help disabled people in these aspects of life.

Some requests for help come from parents and schools and, in response, scooters, tricycles and trolleys have been made for severely disabled children.

A young man in his early twenties who suffers from athetoid cerebral palsy, who has only partial use of one arm and is subject to uncontrolled compulsive movements, achieved little at school. However, with the help of staff at Stevenage College of Further Education, a computer and a REMAP engineer, he has overcome his difficulties sufficiently to be working for O level computer studies.

In Brent, the MSC referred a young man also suffering from athetoid cerebral palsy. Speech and handwriting were impossible for him, but he graduated from Reading University and pursued a postgraduate course at Sussex University. Now, with computer aids, he is working as a journalist and is writing a book. REMAP has made an electrically operated carousel which enables him to consult numerous books without handling them. Other aids have assisted a guitarist who lost his right hand in an accident, and a young chemist with Still's disease who had been unable to remove the tops from bottles.

If you have a problem to which there might be an engineering solution, write to REMAP at their head office, or contact your local branch.

British Telecom

British Telecom has particular 'care and concern' for disabled customers and offers a programme, British Telecom Action for Disabled Customers. As part of the action it has produced a comprehensive guide to equipment and services for disabled customers, and this is freely available to disabled customers and those who work with them. Simply dial 100 and ask for Freefone Telecom Sales, make your request and give your name and address, and your copy of the beautifully presented booklet will be speedily on its way.

There is no need to describe all the Telecom equipment available, as all the information is given in the booklet and the answer to every possible query seems to be clearly set out.

Communication and business aids

Many of the modern communication aids have been mentioned in Chapter 9, but in addition to those that enable disabled people to find employment, there are many other technological innovations that make life easier for disabled people at home. PRESTEL is worth considering, with its enormous store of information on travel, entertainment, shopping, weather, and many other useful subjects. There are also services that enable banking, mail-order shopping, and other financial transactions to be carried out at home.

To use this type of equipment it is not necessary to be able to type; you do not have to know about computers; it is not essential to speak into a telephone or to listen to a voice. The information you request comes up on your TV screen when you dial the appropriate number. The RNIB can advise on devices for magnification or braille transcription.

The range of services available through systems such as PRESTEL is rapidly expanding. News about these services is given in *Soundbarrier* and other disability magazines.

For details of Telebanking, contact the Bank of Scotland, Uberior House, 61 Grassmarket, Edinburgh EH1 3JF on 031-442 7777 and ask for the Home and Office Banking service. For personal accounts there is a monthly subscription fee.

A keyboard terminal for sending messages through these systems costs about £200. You can obtain information and prices from Tandata Marketing Ltd.

The National Association of Deafened People has set up a subcommittee for telecommunications, and they are collecting information to help deaf people to find out about the full range of new aids available, such as electronic mail. They also seek to increase support for research into communication aids, equipment, and services for deafened people. Although such work has deaf and deafened people particularly in mind, those with other disabilities could benefit from the research and technological advances in the communications field.

Communication Aids Centres
There are six centres set up by the DHSS for people with

impaired speech and language skills. Each centre holds a range of demonstration aids, and people who visit the centres (by appointment) are assessed and sometimes loaned aids to see if they are able to use them comfortably.

I have seen young women with no speech using communication equipment from the Charing Cross Hospital Centre. Having this equipment seems to have transformed their lives because they can converse by means of the keyboard and screen. Those unable to use fingers and hands can exert pressure on keys with other parts of the body — for instance with elbows — and communicate via a screen.

A list of these centres is given in the British Telecom guide described on page 124. The Charing Cross Hospital Centre serves London and the surrounding area. Other centres are listed in Chapter 14.

Help from animals

The work of Guide Dogs for the Blind is well known and respected, and any registered blind person or their representative should contact the Association if they would like to know more about the scheme. Guide dogs usually travel free when with blind people.

Less widely known are Hearing Dogs for the Deaf. Concessions such as free travel on British Rail and on National Bus Company vehicles are allowed for the hearing dogs, and they are given free six-monthly checks by a veterinary surgeon.

Specially trained dogs have been successfully placed with a profoundly deaf couple who have a baby and are alerted to the baby's cry by the dog. One dog has been a companion to a deaf/blind elderly lady, and another assists a wheelchair-bound deaf man. A young deaf woman who works for the BBC had a flashing light to alert her when she was needed, but when she was absorbed in her work she did not notice it. Now, with a hearing dog who barks to attract her attention when the light flashes, she has more confidence and has been promoted to be a researcher.

So far, 24 hearing dogs have been placed, and they are easily recognised by their orange collars and leads. For further details of the scheme, or with offers of support for this new charity, write to Hearing Dogs for the Deaf.

Help from trade unions

If you are eligible for membership of a trade union or professional association, it could be to your advantage to join. You may be glad of their support in any dispute with your employer, and most unions have benevolent funds, convalescent and holiday centres, and other social services from which you could benefit.

The Trades Union Congress (TUC) encourages union representatives to ensure that employers meet their quota requirements, that disabled people are given equal job opportunities, and that their special needs are met. Representatives should be aware of the Disablement Advisory Service provisions, and be ready to advise both employers and employees about these.

It is important that disabled people should play their part in unions so as to promote the interests of disabled workers, as well as taking part in union activities on equal terms with other members. The TUC Guide on the Employment of Disabled People suggests, 'if shop stewards or other union representatives do not include someone who is disabled, a disabled member might be co-opted for discussions on matters relating to disabled workers.' It also stresses that meetings should be held in places accessible to disabled members and that 'assistance should be given to enable blind or deaf members to take part in meetings'.

Be prepared to take office in a union, not only to speak for disabled members, but because as a disabled member you have the same responsibilities as other able-bodied members.

In addition to the appropriate union for each industry or profession, there is also the National League of the Blind and Disabled, which is affiliated to the TUC and the Scottish TUC. One of the special services this union offers members is legal assistance in accident cases.

Anyone who is able-bodied, or who uses a wheelchair on the pavements, must often have noticed holes and obstructions of potential danger, particularly to visually handicapped people. Unfortunately, accidents do occur through these hazards, and though the League usually wins cases it takes up on behalf of members injured in this way, it would be better still if the accidents were prevented! Report hazards to the local council, and keep the pavements safe for blind and disabled people.

Organisations

There are a great many organisations concerned with the well-being of disabled people. Some have already been mentioned in this book, but the following may have relevant services for people seeking a career.

The Spastics Society

The Society has a small team of Careers Advisory Officers who work in liaison with local authority Careers Advisory Officers to help young people with cerebral palsy plan their future. They give advice on further education, training, and employment.

The Society also has a well stocked resource centre where aids, equipment, toys, and literature can be inspected. Although the emphasis is on children, problems faced by disabled adults are also given attention. Before visiting the centre, telephone 01-636 5020 to make an appointment. You will receive a friendly welcome.

The Association for Spina Bifida and Hydrocephalus (ASBAH)

The Society has an experienced staff who are ready to help with any problems relating to those with spina bifida or hydrocephalus.

There are nearly 100 branches throughout the country, and they are listed in the Association's lively bi-monthly magazine, *Link*. Anyone with a child who has spina bifida or hydrocephalus would certainly be wise to join this caring organisation. Alterations to the home, education, the provision of aids and equipment, occupation and employment, are among their concerns. 'Towards Independence' is their motto, and the aim of all their work. The Association also publishes a booklet called 'Making Our Way'.

The Royal Society for Mentally Handicapped Children and Adults

Many people with handicapped children have good cause to be thankful for this Society which has pioneered so many schemes for the education, training, and employment of mentally handicapped youngsters, and fought for their right to have a say in their own future. Local groups offer warm, friendly, mutual support to parents and to those who work with the children. The MENCAP Pathway Employment scheme is also in operation (see Chapter 2). Those needing advice or help concerning a young handicapped person should contact MENCAP.

The Muscular Dystrophy Group
Though mainly concerned with research into the cause, treatment and cure of this and allied neuromuscular diseases, the Group also helps those who suffer from this disease, and it publishes excellent explanatory literature.

The Parkinson's Disease Society
This Society was formed by patients, relatives and friends because they felt there was a great lack of information on the disease and the problems it brings. In a letter to me, the Welfare Benefits Officer said: 'Our Society receives many requests from people whose Parkinsonism brings their original career to a premature end.' The Society publishes booklets and a newsletter, and gives information on the nature of the disease, its treatment, and advice on how best to cope with the disability.

The Spinal Injuries Association
This friendly, informal organisation works by introducing people to each other, so that someone who has suffered an injury can be encouraged by hearing how another person is coping with similar disabilities. The charity is run by people who are paraplegic or tetraplegic.

Local councils and associations for the disabled
In many areas there are regional and local associations that act as umbrella organisations and sources of information. For instance, the Wales Council for the Disabled has a most comprehensive annual guide, *Factfinder*, in English and Welsh, listing all the local MPs, House of Lords Members, Health Authorities, DHSS Offices, District Planning Officers, Community Health Councils, Disablement Resettlement Services, and all manner of local organisations and charities working for or with disabled people. It is invaluable for disabled people and their families living in Wales.

Chapter 11

Mobility

The one single factor that makes an enormous difference to life for many disabled people is having a car and being able to drive it. Employment, family and social life, and hospital treatment or rehabilitation, are all made so much easier for disabled people who can drive to the place where they want to be at the time they want to be there. If you are disabled and cannot drive, learning to drive should be a high priority, if it is at all possible. People with severe disabilities have learnt to drive ordinary or adapted cars, and this has brought them freedom, independence, and sometimes made employment possible.

Learning to drive

There is now a Mobility Advice and Information Service Centre at Crowthorne, Berkshire, where disabled people can find out for themselves if they could learn to drive, and the type of vehicle that would be most suitable. The Centre is at the government's Transport and Road Research Laboratory, Crowthorne, and it was opened by Mrs Lynda Chalker (when a junior Transport Minister) in the autumn of 1985. 'Without the kind of facilities we are offering, far too many disabled people either are forced into making costly mistakes or, worse still, are so daunted by the problems that they will never drive at all,' said Mrs Chalker at the opening. A wide range of modified vehicles to suit different types of incapacity will be available at Crowthorne for disabled drivers to test in safe off-road conditions. You must hold a full or provisional licence to make an appointment to visit the Centre.

The Mobility Advice and Vehicle Information Service (MAVIS) is funded by the Department of Transport and has other, smaller, mobility centres in Cardiff, Edinburgh and Belfast, as well as a Mobility Information Service based in Telford. Addresses are given in *Door-to-Door* (see page 132).

There has been a recent move to extend the work of Artificial Limb and Appliance Centres (ALAC) to include wheelchair and other mobility aids, especially those designed to enable people to travel up to two miles, so watch out for developments in your area.

At Banstead Place there is a mobility centre — a separate charity linked with Queen Elizabeth's Foundation, Leatherhead, Surrey KT22 0BN, and this is specially geared to young people who want to learn to drive. It has received generous help from the Ford Motor Company.

The British School of Motoring has adapted cars for disabled people who wish to learn to drive, and it runs an assessment centre at 81-87 Hartfield Road, London SW19 3TJ. If you want to discover your nearest BSM with adapted cars, or if you want to be assessed for your driving potential, write to the above address for further information.

Driving lessons are expensive, and so you need to go to a driving school that will give you good value and provide competent instructors. Often it is best to look for the established driving schools with a high reputation. Here again, you will have to ask friends and local disability organisations for advice. Most driving schools offer a trial lesson at a reduced fee. If you do not feel happy with the instructor assigned to you, ask for another or go elsewhere.

Before you have any lessons, help yourself by learning as much as you can about cars, driving, and the Highway Code. You need to understand something about how a car works, and the function of the various controls, before you begin your lessons. There is no point in spending expensive lesson time learning points you could easily have picked up from a book, or from sitting in a car with a friend or relative capable of explaining things to you.

Residential driving courses

You may feel that a few days' thorough, intensive tuition would give you the practice and the confidence you need to bring you to the standard required to pass the driving test. One such centre, with provision for disabled people, is EP Training Services Ltd in Surrey. Look in the English Tourist Board's *Activity and Hobby Holidays* guide for others. Such courses are expensive, but one may be a good investment for you.

Buying a car

As this is one of the largest items of expenditure for most people, it is important to seek the best possible advice and to try as many cars as you can. Ask friends and garages to allow you to sit in different cars. It is essential to find a car that is comfortable for you, one that you can handle and control well, that gives you good visibility, has easy access, and that you can afford to insure, run, and maintain.

If you are in receipt of a Mobility Allowance or a Private Car Allowance, and you are over 18 years of age, you can buy a car outright, with up to 17 per cent discount off the basic list price, through the Motability Scheme (address in Chapter 14), which also offers concessions on hire purchase or leasing. Leading motor manufacturers will tell you what they can offer.

If you decide to buy a second-hand car, it is wise to buy from a reputable garage who will be willing to service the car. Arrange to have an AA or RAC inspection before buying. Remember that once you have put a deposit on a car, you are obliged to buy it or forfeit the deposit.

When you come to insure your car, shop around for the best deal, as some insurance companies may try to weight the premium against you because you are disabled.

The Department of Transport publishes a comprehensive free guide, *Door-to-Door*, which gives information about buying and running a car, and the entitlement to aids and financial benefit. It also includes information about public transport facilities and services for disabled travellers, and is available from disability organisations or from the Department of Transport, Freepost (no stamp required; address in Chapter 14).

Adaptations

Automatic cars enable many disabled drivers to dispense with adaptations and hand controls, but others will require them. A magazine such as *The Disabled Driver*, published by the Disabled Drivers' Motor Club, carries advertisements and editorial describing different equipment and systems of hand controls. Study these to see the range available, and the names and addresses of your nearest stockists.

Health authorities sometimes arrange day seminars on various aspects of driving for disabled people. The programme includes assessment, learning to drive, safety, and finance. Such a day, held at Bath University, was organised around an exhibition of special vehicles.

Ask the Disabled Drivers' Motor Club for the address of your nearest local area representative, who will know about such events and will be a good person to give you advice on purchasing and adapting a car.

Club membership is well worth while for every disabled driver or learner-driver. For details, write to DDMC Membership Bureau, Freepost, Coventry CV2 3BR.

Parking

All the provisions about parking concessions for disabled and blind people are outlined in a leaflet, 'The Orange Badge Scheme', published by the Department of Transport and the Central Office of Information. Orange badges are issued by the local authority to individuals who have a severe handicap. Not all disabled people are eligible for a badge.

Some local authorities allow concessionary parking only to those motorists who hold an additional badge which they issue to local residents or to people who work in their area. When you go to a different part of the country, make sure that you comply with the local parking regulations. Ask about their car park concessions.

London Regional Transport

A new leaflet, 'Access to the Underground', price 50p from LRT Unit for Disabled Passengers, 55 Broadway, London SW1H 0BD, would be of interest to anyone able to use stairs, but not escalators. The leaflet admits that only 20 out of 272 London Transport stations have fewer than 20 steps between entrance and platform!

Mobility allowance

DHSS leaflet NI 211 gives general guidance on Mobility Allowance and how to set about claiming it. Ask your local DHSS office for a copy, or send for one from the DHSS Leaflets Unit. 'Help for Handicapped People', Leaflet HB1, gives notes on many benefits. On 25 November 1985, the Secretary of State for Social Services told Parliament that 400,400 people were receiving mobility allowance. He added: 'I regret that it is not possible to give estimates of take-up (of benefits), in view of uncertainties about the numbers of people entitled to use these benefits.' Study the literature, consult the DHSS, and see if you would be entitled to receive this valuable benefit.

Remember that you do not have to be able to drive to receive mobility allowance. It can be spent in any way that will help you get out and about. Local authority taxi-fare concession schemes are proving a boon to severely disabled people, like John, an Oxford graduate incapacitated by multiple sclerosis. He undertakes book jacket design and reviewing, and uses the taxi-card service when he visits publishers. In common with other severely disabled people, he finds public transport in London impossible to use.

Other disabled people are glad to use the mobility allowance towards the cost of running a family car. Sian, in Wales, already mentioned in this book, is very disappointed that she seems unable to learn to drive. This is partly because she lives in an isolated place and finds it difficult to reach the nearest large town where she could have regular driving lessons, but also because she has concentration problems. She therefore uses her mobility allowance to get out and about by train, and to help keep her father's car on the road so that he can take her out.

Janet, who wrote to me from Cornwall, is one of the disabled people who is able to work largely because she can drive. 'I had a diving accident when I was 14 and broke my neck. I have some use in my right leg, I can use my right hand, my triceps are weak, my biceps quite good and my shoulders have become very strongly developed. Over the years driving and various sports have strengthened my muscles, improved my balance etc, but it is a slow business.

'I had my accident while at a boarding school and after a year in hospital I returned there. When I left school I took a course in proof-reading . . . now I am working for a firm of colour-printers.

'I drive to work in my car. Someone gets me in, in my wheelchair. Once inside the offices I transfer to an electric wheelchair supplied by the DHSS. The firm have put up a rail in the toilet and I manage OK. In the evening someone gets me out into my car. I have been there ten years. Incidentally, when writing I form the letters from my shoulder, not my wrist. That isn't really why this letter is so badly written (it was in fact very neat), that is because I am getting a lot of pain in my arm at the moment.'

Chapter 12

Using Your Spare Time Creatively

Disabled people who are unable to find paid employment are like millions of other unemployed people — they have spare time. There are as many different ways of spending this leisure as there are individuals. The important thing seems to be that it should be used and enjoyed.

You may feel that all you want to do is use your time and energy to search for a job or profitable way of using your skills. For some that will be the best choice.

Others may want to think how they can enjoy the free time their situation gives them. They may have had a demanding working life, suddenly halted by accident or injury so that now, quite unexpectedly, they are at leisure to follow their own interests or find new ones. Loss of a job for any reason — sickness, redundancy, business failure — can be agonising and seemingly catastrophic, but it can also be liberating. The main problem is that often there is little money with which to enjoy this newly acquired liberty. Here are some suggestions for leisure activities that do not necessarily involve great expense.

Learning

In these days of high unemployment there is increased provision for people to widen their education, study a specific subject or learn new skills. Though they may not be designed as paths to employment, classes, lectures, and courses can lead to new career opportunities as well as aiding personal fulfilment. See what your local authority offers at adult institutes and further education colleges, and consider some of the other methods of learning mentioned in Chapter 5.

Find out about purely leisure interest classes too. Perhaps a local Flower Arrangement Society, a Local History Group or National Trust branch has a programme of lectures you would enjoy. A community centre may have a women's group which meets very informally to learn more about healthy eating or self-help, for example; a local church may have an occasional course of lectures or discussion groups.

Watch the local papers, look at the notices in the library and in the windows of shops and offices, such as CABs, the Community Health Council and Consumer Advisory Centres, to see what is happening locally.

Hobbies

You may at last have time to pursue some special interest or take up a new one. In most places there are clubs and groups of people who come together with a common enthusiasm for gardening, trains, stamps, coins, archaeology, jazz and so on. It is amazing how much activity there is in some areas.

Joining a mixed group of people brought together by a common interest may demand some initial courage, but it could be of great benefit. It is good to get to know a new circle of people; when you meet a fellow cactus-grower, or racing pigeon owner, you are on equal terms — you have a particular interest in common. This is why many disabled people enjoy such organisations more than groups specifically for the disabled. People who are disabled in some way, or in wheelchairs, do not necessarily have much else in common. Although there is much to be said for the mutual support and understanding such groups offer, it seems a mistake to limit one's social life to organisations for disabled people. 'The last thing I want to do is spend time with other sufferers from my condition,' explained Jef, a civil servant who walked with the aid of two sticks. However, he found the Disabled Drivers' Motor Club a great help.

'We try to encourage the youngsters to go to ordinary local youth groups,' said the project leader at one community living unit for disabled young people, 'but they don't find it easy.' That project is particularly concerned about integration because many of the youngsters there have spent all their schooldays and holidays with other disabled young people. The leader now runs an annual holiday for disabled and able-bodied youngsters together; this has been of value for all, and led to better understanding. If you are the parent of a disabled young person, encourage your child to mix with non-disabled youngsters.

Of course, organisations for people with disabilities do have their place; the members can work together to increase public awareness of problems such as poor access to public buildings and inadequate services, as well as enjoying group activities and outings. It is entirely a matter of choice. If you want to join a disabled persons' group, ask your local social services to tell you about those that would be suitable for you. Once you join one group, other members will probably tell you about all the various groups to which they are attached. For you, this may be the way of making the most of your leisure, of gaining new friends, and of encouraging and helping other disabled people.

Organisations

Local branches of national organisations, such as the Women's Institute, Townswomen's Guild, the Royal British Legion and other ex-forces associations, the Housewives' Register, the Trefoil Guild (for former Guides and Guiders), may appeal to you. See which groups meet in an accessible place; maybe members could offer you help with transport or with getting into the building. Belonging to such an organisation will help keep your outlook wide, and its conferences and courses may give you a chance to travel to other parts of the UK or abroad.

Choirs, musical appreciation and drama groups could be another source of pleasure and new friendships. Disability may not prevent you from singing or playing a musical instrument and, if you enjoy music, only deafness may make a musical appreciation group or class inappropriate.

Even if you do not feel able to act, you could help with prompting, advertising and ticket selling for a drama group's performances. Some groups spend time just reading plays; this is something those with clear speech may do well, especially if they have the time to study the play carefully beforehand.

Churches

Those who have time to think and ponder, and perhaps to read the Bible or other religious books, according to their religion, and pray, may decide they want to take their religion more seriously and join a church, if they do not belong to one already. Being part of an active, worshipping community is a great strength and encouragement. You will be with people committed to a faith you want to share, or at least explore.

Sadly, some churches were built when flights of steps to the front entrance were a popular feature, and access by disabled people was not carefully considered. However, more churches are now installing ramps, or there may be a side door that allows easier access.

If you join a church, try to play your full part, and take your share of the jobs to be done. There may be linen or books that require mending, typing that needs doing for the magazine, or perhaps you could visit someone in the parish who feels lonely or depressed. You want to be treated as a normal member of the congregation — not as a 'special case' to be fussed over. Be responsible about your giving, too.

If you cannot get up to the communion rail don't worry, communion will be brought to you. Maybe a friend will sit beside you for this so that you do not feel lonely or different from everyone else.

You may be interested to know that there is one particular religious order especially for women who feel that they have a vocation to the contemplative life, but suffer a disability that prevents them entering most convents. The order has a comfortable guest house with ground floor accommodation for those who want a quiet holiday or retreat. Details from the Guest Mistress, Sisters of Jesus Crucified, St John's Priory, Castle Cary, Somerset BA7 7PF.

Serving the community

No one likes receiving all the time — it can be one of the frustrating aspects of illness or disability. As well as aiming for independence, think what you could do to help others, either on your own or through an organisation.

- Perhaps you can play a leading part in a tenants' or residents' association, or do some of the chores attached to any such society.
- Is there someone living near you who has a child who would like some help with reading, or who just needs a little individual attention from someone prepared to sit and talk and listen?
- Is there a lonely, old person you could visit, or with whom you could have occasional telephone chats?
- Can you knit or sew for any organisation needing blankets or baby clothes?
- Could you re-constitute greetings cards to sell for a charity's funds?

- Can you make picture books for teachers to use with severely mentally disadvantaged children? Ask a school or residential home exactly what they need.
- Can you make or mend toys and books for any play-group or school?
- Could you counsel a disabled person — perhaps someone who is newly disabled and finds it hard to come to terms with the situation?
- Can you invite a few lonely people, just two or three at a time, to meet in your home?
- Have you equipment or adaptations that it would be a help for other disabled people to see? Could you assist them to make something similar if it would be useful for them?
- Can you help to set up or run a group for which there seems to be local need?
- Are there lonely people who would appreciate a letter from you? There are organisations, such as Amnesty International, that need people to write to dissidents and others in prison, or to foreign governments on behalf of prisoners. Advice can be obtained from Amnesty International. Could you do this?
- Is there a charity or organisation near you that would be glad of voluntary help in the office?
- Is there a community centre that needs helpers?
- Perhaps there is a local charity shop where you could help? If selling is rather tiring, there are other jobs you might do, such as sorting out the jewellery, buttons and oddments, and mounting these on cards.
- Is there a stately home, local museum, interpretive centre, or some other tourist attraction that needs volunteer guides or bookstall helpers? One of the liveliest and most informative guides I have ever encountered was a physically disabled lady who led parties round the ground floor of Wilton House.
- Is there a local geriatric ward, old people's home, or some other institution where visitors from the outside world would be welcome? Most people confined to a hospital or institution are glad to see different faces and chat with someone new.

If you have any particular skills, perhaps you could sing, play or demonstrate a craft to a group? A simple game of cards with someone may help to pass the time for him or her. Sometimes people are glad of someone who will write a letter for them. It may be that you know just one person who is in an institution and needs a friend. The chaplain may be able to tell you of someone who has no family and would welcome a personal visitor.

Hospitals also need helpers in shops, canteens and libraries; these may be the spot where you could help.

Loneliness is one of the quiet, unseen forms of suffering. People experience it on housing estates, in tall blocks of flats, in comfortable suburban settings, and in villages too. If you can offer friendship, companionship, a helping hand to just one other person, you will be helping to combat one of the greatest social problems of today. Often people do not want or need a professional social worker — they want friends, and they need to be drawn into a group. Of course, some people are perfectly self-contained, they do not want others to intrude on their lives, but innate common sense should tell you when this is the case.

As a disabled person you may have special knowledge and skills you want to share with other disabled people. This is certainly true of David and Jean Griffiths, featured in 'Making Our Way'. They work voluntarily three days a week for the Mobility Information Service.

Finding where you are needed
A local Citizens' Advice Bureau may be able to tell you about organisations that need volunteers. Sometimes local papers and magazines carry appeals for help, or invitations to join a circle concerned with some particular problem or group of people. The Volunteer Centre at Berkhamsted may have some ideas for you. In the magazine *New Society* there is now a page where voluntary organisations can advertise their need for helpers. The particular voluntary jobs you see mentioned there may not be realistic possibilities for you, but they could give you ideas to pursue.

Benefit position
Some voluntary work carries small payments to cover expenses and provide pocket money. If you are receiving unemployment benefit, this could be affected if you earn above the minimum currently allowed. To check on your position, study the DHSS leaflet, 'Voluntary Work and Social Security Benefits', or ask your benefit office for advice. If you are working for a charity,

check that they have insurance to cover accidents.

Money raising

Most charities are conscious of work that needs doing, and opportunities that they could take — if only they had sufficient money. Almost inevitably, you will be drawn into money-raising activities if you are involved in any charity. Try to be imaginative and think of new things you could do or make. When you make things for sale, or encourage other people to do this, insist on good design, materials worthy of the effort, and high standards of workmanship. No one wants people to buy items out of pity; you want them to buy things because they are attractive and useful.

If you make toys, do check that they are safe and conform to safety standards. Avoid eyes that can be pulled out, trimmings that can be nibbled and swallowed, ribbons that are loose, sharp edges and rough surfaces. There is now much more awareness of the need for safety in commercial toy production, but a child could still choke on a toy sold at a charity fair.

Sponsored activities are a popular form of fund-raising, but don't overdo this method. Try to look for some positive action, such as tidying up an open space, or knitting squares for blankets, rather than just swimming lengths or walking footpaths.

Marathons seem to be an exception; people recognise the effort involved, especially when it is made by disabled people, and they will sponsor on miles or speed. By their walking, swimming or wheelchair travels, many disabled people make a great contribution to charity funds. If you feel able to make such an effort, go ahead and look for sponsors. You could always suggest that sponsors promise to pay up to an agreed maximum amount — then they will not be faced with a request for an unexpectedly large sum.

Small, regular weekly or monthly giving can bring in large amounts and be a reliable source of income for a charity, if enough people are prepared to participate. Collecting the weekly 10p can provide opportunities for maintaining interest and giving supporters up-to-date news about the charity or project.

The Children's Society gains considerable income from 'collectables', such as badges, buttons, and old lace, that supporters give for sale through auctions or charity shops. Perhaps your home could become a 'depot' for similar items that your charity could collect and sell for funds?

Mail order catalogues produced by charities are another useful means of money-raising, especially before Christmas.

It can be fun to join in money-raising activities such as concerts, fêtes and sales, and even if your mobility is restricted there is likely to be something you can do to help. So don't be shy, lend a hand and show that disabled people are willing to do their share of work for others.

Physical recreation

There are all kinds of physical recreation that a disabled person can enjoy and use as an opportunity for making friends. I know one married couple who met through the kidney patients' 'Olympics'. Here are some of the sports and games that attract disabled people: archery, angling, boating, bowling, canoeing, fencing, golf, riding, sailing, swimming.

The RADAR *Directory for Disabled People* includes many addresses of organisations that give advice on these activities. There seems little point in repeating them all here, and they do often change, so it is difficult to keep up to date. If you want to know how you can join in any of these sports, write to the British Paraplegic Sports Society. It exists 'to bring the joys of sport and physical recreation to people, young and old, with many different kinds of disability'. The Society is recognised by the government and the Sports Council as the co-ordinating body for 'all types of sport for all types of disablement'. For addresses, and advice on aids and equipment, write to the Society. The Centre has a large sports hall, swimming pool, indoor bowls green, and other facilities. If you live near enough, it would be worth seeing if you could take advantage of these.

Apart from the BPS, and organisations concerned with promoting particular sports, there are the Scottish Sports Association for the Disabled; the Northern Ireland Paraplegic Association that organises paraplegic games; PHAB organisation (Physically Handicapped and Able-Bodied) that 'seeks to extend the opportunities for physically handicapped people to enjoy a wide range of leisure and recreational activities alongside able-bodied members'; and the Welsh Sports Association for the Disabled. For the addresses of these and other bodies consult RADAR or any local disability organisation that is likely to have comprehensive directories, and Chapter 14.

Gardening

Although gardening may not be an obvious hobby choice for a disabled person, remember you don't have to dig or weed. You can create a garden on a window sill, balcony, patio, or in tubs. Any home is enhanced by plants. As a disabled person, you may well spend a considerable amount of time at home, so make it attractive and welcoming with herbs, flowering plants, miniature trees, bulbs, African violets, foliage plants — or whatever appeals to you, and that you can grow easily.

It is fun to be an expert on something; so if you are fascinated by a particular plant, why not specialise in growing it? When my son was visiting people for a council housing survey he came home one day quite excited by the plants a pensioner had shown him. He immediately started tidying up and re-potting our own house plants: enthusiasm is catching!

Outdoor gardening does not have to be too ambitious. Aim for plenty of colour where you can see it from the living room. A few thickly planted little beds can be as effective as a long border — and a lot less tiring to maintain.

The RHS demonstration gardens at Wisley show what can be done from a wheelchair, and how garden beds can be raised for easier cultivation. Gardens for the Disabled Trust in Kent offers advice on garden design, aids for easier gardening, and a quarterly newsletter that encourages disabled gardeners to exchange plants.

There is no need to go to great expense with special adaptations. Think about any outdoor space you have and consider how you can make the most of it. Just a pot of brilliant nasturtiums is a cheering sight, while giant sunflowers always arouse interest. Cress and lettuce seedlings are easy to grow. It is also worth thinking of growing for scent; pleasant smells can be therapeutic. For a simple start, why not try a hyacinth bulb planted in fibre, or balanced on a glass vase?

Gardening catalogues are colourful and often free, so send for some of those advertised in your newspaper, browse through them and see what you could grow.

Indoor games

Bridge, chess, scrabble, whist, and numerous card and board games can be enjoyed at home, or in a club or institution. Playing games can be a distraction from pain and discomfort, an exercise in thought and concentration, and fun. Children learn through playing games, and sharing the excitement of a game can unite a family group. Monopoly is an old favourite, while Trivial Pursuit has caught on fast. Snakes and ladders, ludo, or Chinese chequers can happily be played by a group of mixed ages and abilities, so have one or two of these games handy when children come to visit you.

If you go to a day centre or social club you might like to take along one or two of your games, and suggest that other members bring some too. Beetle drives or whist could provide entertainment for a few sessions, and perhaps raise a little money for funds.

Some readers may be keen chess or bridge players, and be willing to teach others or start a regular group. Those who take these games seriously may want to go on the bridge or chess weekends which are sometimes advertised in enthusiasts' magazines.

Jigsaw puzzles are a pleasant pastime, and sitting peacefully working at one can be therapeutic for someone convalescing or feeling depressed. There is a British Jigsaw Library (established in 1933) in Herefordshire. Jigsaw enthusiasts could arrange to swap puzzles, or take one along to a club or day centre.

Don't forget there is Bingo too, if you want somewhere to go and be with other people. It may even be cheaper than using heating at home.

Entertainments

Often disabled people are offered concessionary prices, so take advantage of these. You will soon discover which local theatres, cinemas or halls are easiest for you.

In London, with help from the Greater London Council, SHAPE has been able to negotiate concessionary prices for the London Zoo and London theatres. Its volunteer escorts and drivers have enabled many disabled people to take advantage of free entertainments or reduced price tickets. One ticket scheme user said: 'I feel as if I have been liberated: it is marvellous to be able to plan something for oneself and to share one's enjoyment with other people.' How far SHAPE will be able to continue their service without GLC support is not clear at the moment. But it would be worthwhile for disabled people in London to check what help is currently available. Those who run clubs for disabled people in other parts of the country may want to see if they can initiate similar local schemes.

Holidays

Everyone benefits from a good holiday — not least disabled people. There is all manner of special provision by charities and trusts too numerous to mention in this book. It would be easiest to obtain details from RADAR or other organisations for disabled people. The RADAR *Directory for Disabled People* contains a good collection of helpful addresses.

Consult the RADAR annual guide, *Holidays for Disabled People*, for lists of hotels offering accommodation for disabled people. Those hotels that have been visited for RADAR are indicated; others have been included on the strength of information supplied by owners or managers, so before booking you may want to check for yourself that they are suitable. The AA also issues a comprehensive *Guide for the Disabled Traveller*. The English and Scottish Tourist Boards' guides indicate the properties that are suitable for disabled people.

When you have decided which area of the country, or which resort you would like to visit, do not hesitate to consult the appropriate tourist board or office. They will be pleased to give you advice — attracting visitors to that area is their business. Any of the 700 Tourist Information Centres will tell you the address and telephone number of the office you may want to contact.

Apart from holiday homes and centres which are equipped and intended solely for disabled people and their families, there is growing awareness of the importance of providing for disabled people in ordinary hotels, and on package holidays. Launching the latest edition of *Providing for Disabled Visitors*, published by the English Tourist Board and Holiday Care Service, the Rt Hon Norman Tebbit MP said: 'The disabled are increasing in numbers, and together with their families they represent substantial purchasing power . . . but there are fewer than 300 hotel bedrooms in the UK designed for their use. The hotel industry can and must do more to cater for its disabled clients in all parts of the country and in all price ranges.'

The ETB attaches great importance to holiday provision for disabled people. Mr Duncan Bluck, chairman of the ETB, announced at the launch: '. . . facilities for disabled people, including the extra costs that this provision often demands, will be given priority in requests for assistance under Section 4 of the Development of Tourism Act.'

The Holiday Care Service gives disabled people free information and advice about holidays. Write to them or telephone explaining what kind of holiday you want, and they will suggest appropriate places, leaving you to make the booking yourself.

The ETB publications, such as *Farm Holidays*, *England's Seaside* and *Activity and Hobby Holidays*, use symbols to indicate hotels and guest houses suitable for disabled people, or they include a separate list.

However, before you book, you should check that the place will be suitable for your particular needs. Is there a ramp or level entrance for wheelchairs? Are doorways wide enough, and lifts large enough? Are toilet facilities suitable? Look for a place that has a pleasant terrace, solarium, or balcony where you can sit in a warm or sheltered spot and enjoy the view. Anyone can find a hotel or guest house disappointing — that 'two minutes from the sea' seems further than you expected — so look at the brochure photographs carefully, and check with the local tourist board if in doubt.

The Scottish and Welsh Tourist Boards are also keen to make good provision for disabled visitors, so don't hesitate to ask for their advice.

Some people will want to use a holiday not just for rest and recreation, but as a chance to learn. The *Activity and Hobby Holidays* guide includes holidays devoted to a great variety of special interests, from amateur radio and astrology to philosophy, theology and social studies. Some will see these courses as a chance of improving their expertise and helping them to make a saleable product; relevant courses include pottery, etching, calligraphy, and weaving. Millfield Village of Education in Somerset offers 342 separate courses for people of all ages. The Director writes: 'We make every effort to welcome anyone whose disabilities do not preclude them.' There are special integration courses for young, hearing-impaired people.

Holiday centres

People who are severely disabled may well feel more confident if they go to a holiday centre designed for disabled people and run by experienced, skilled staff. At some of these centres there are low cost holidays. Sometimes local authorities or charities will give a grant to enable a disabled person to have a holiday at a special centre. The organisations that run such holiday centres are too numerous to list here. To find one suited to your needs, consult members of any disability organisation to which you belong, local social services, and magazines and directories for disabled people.

A disabled person's enterprise
Jennie and Bob Donaldson's Gorslwyd Farm in Dyfed has five comfortable self-catering cottages, purpose built for disabled people. The whole site has been landscaped and carefully planned so that disabled people can enjoy the lovely woodland setting. There are imaginative features such as a barbecue area, an adventure play area, and a craft workshop. This centre fulfilled Jennie and Bob's ambition to create a holiday centre for disabled people, because Bob, who is in a wheelchair, realised the difficulties encountered by families with a disabled member.

Caravan and camping
For caravan and camping holidays, consult guides issued by the clubs and societies concerned with these activities. David and Jean Griffiths, already mentioned in this book and featured in 'Making Our Way', are keen caravan campers. David has camped in many parts of Britain and Europe, and two years ago he started Camping for the Disabled, which he runs with the help of his wife. They provide members with information about accessible sites. They have found that when they go to camp sites, other campers are invariably helpful. You can write to David Griffiths c/o Coptherne Community Hall, Shelton Road, Shewsbury SY3 8TD.

Travel
Magazines produced by disability organisations often contain amazing accounts of journeys made by people in wheelchairs. 'Have Wheels Will Travel' was the motto for one couple who visited Hawaii and Puerto Rico. They described their holiday in the same issue of 'Contact', the RADAR quarterly magazine, as a RADAR committee member wrote about her two-week holiday in Texas. She commented how greatly station and airport services had improved for wheelchair travellers in recent years: 'the Gatwick Express has special facilities for those in wheelchairs . . . and both the boarding and flight went fine.'

If you are really determined to travel, and have sufficient money and an able-bodied friend or relative to accompany

147

you, there seems to be no limit to the travelling disabled people can, and do, enjoy. Ask travel agents which companies offer good facilities for disabled travellers and which produce helpful preparatory literature. Some travel companies say that they specialise in holidays for disabled people, but before you book, talk to someone who has travelled with them. You want to be sure that the company is reliable and really does understand your needs.

In RADAR's *Directory for Disabled People* there is good advice for intending air travellers, and notes about the services offered by individual airlines. But as addresses and services change frequently, you need to ask RADAR for a list of the most recent leaflets available: please enclose an sae.

Notes entitled 'Care in the Air', giving details of special airport facilities for disabled air travellers, is obtainable free of charge from the Secretary, Air Transport Users Committee, 129 Kingsway, London WC2B 6NN.

When going on holiday abroad, one of the most difficult and relatively costly parts of the journey can be travel to and from the airport. If you intend to drive to an airport and park there while you are away, it is worth finding out if there are any concessions for disabled drivers. Last summer we found that we could park in the short-stay car park at Luton terminal at the long-stay rates charged in more distant parking areas. It was extremely easy to get from this short-stay parking area to the departure lounge, and there was no need to climb stairs or travel on an escalator.

In London, a new busline called Careline is due to start in 1986. It will operate an hourly bus service from Victoria to all the Heathrow terminals. The vehicles used will be single-decker buses with some seats removed for wheelchairs, and there will be a hoist for loading wheelchairs on to the bus. Details can be obtained from Alder Valley Services. This company also has coaches for eight wheelchair and 20 seated passengers for group travel.

Cross-Channel services
Disabled drivers who plan to cross the Channel should contact organisations for disabled drivers, and consult British Rail and channel ferry operators to discover what facilities they offer for disabled drivers and passengers. One disabled driver, Edith, writing in the *Disabled Driver*, says: 'We always sail with Townsend Thoresen via Portsmouth as this particular

ferry company goes out of its way to help disabled travellers. All it requires is a note to the boarding officer informing him of the date and time of travel, and he will position your car as close to the lift as possible. The stewards are most helpful . . .' She goes on to add that the French Tourist Office will provide lists of hotels in two chains that offer en suite bedrooms on the ground floor.

If you are thinking of a continental holiday, do make enquiries and bookings in good time. Some concessions cannot be obtained at the last moment.

Rail travel

For information about facilities for disabled travellers, and for a list of destinations served by trains with removable seat facilities for wheelchair users, obtain a copy of the free leaflet, 'British Rail and Disabled Travellers', at main line stations or at BR Travel Centres.

Special courses

The Spastics Society careers advisory staff recently organised their second residential, 'Alternative Lifestyles Course'. Eighteen unemployed, physically disabled young people, aged between 20 and 35, travelled to Hereward College, Coventry, for the four-day conference.

Sue Hennessy, careers advisory officer to the Spastics Society, wrote in *Handicapped Living*: 'The organisers hoped that by participating in a wide range of leisure and recreational activities, and by listening to the ideas and experiences of invited speakers, the course members would gain both the inspiration and the confidence to reorganise their time in a more stimulating and satisfying way.'

The course members sampled activities such as riding, local history, crafts and gardening, that they had not previously attempted, and they spent a whole day pursuing a new interest in depth. On offer were photography, introduction to home computers, printmaking, and cooking for friends. The computer sessions were particularly helpful for a number of people who had bought computers but did not know how to use them. At the end of the day, the group leaders explained how each activity could be followed up at home.

One of the most popular lectures was on the subject of earning money from home. People listened intently as the speaker suggested ways to fill the gaps in the market and thereby find satisfying work and a modest income. The Spastics Society hopes that all who participated will have carried away new enthusiasms that they will want to share with others.

This course sounds very worthwhile; perhaps an organisation to which you belong could arrange something similar. It is important that people who are unemployed should be encouraged to make the best possible use of their time.

Writing

Writing can be a pleasant, absorbing occupation for anyone, and those who enjoy writing and have time to practise it are fortunate. If they really want to write, there is nothing to stop them. How many times have you heard someone say, 'I would like to write a book one day . . .' But often it remains a dream; they never sit down and begin the work. If you want to write, start today. Once you have begun, it can be easy. For many people, getting started is the great difficulty.

There are many books on writing, and on earning money by writing. Look for them in your public library. *The Writers' and Artists' Year Book* is useful, but do use an up-to-date copy; *Writing for a Living* may also be of help.

If you want to write an article for a magazine, study the publication thoroughly before you begin to write, and observe the content and style. Write about what you know. Give facts and figures, as well as opinions. Send a neat copy of your manuscript to the publisher (with an sae), and keep a copy. Don't be discouraged when a manuscript is returned; study it carefully and try to think why it was rejected. Most editors do not explain why they are returning a manuscript. Perhaps the magazine has already published an article on the topic you have chosen, or it may be that you have not written the piece well enough, or in the right style.

Many towns have writers' clubs and circles, and you may like to join one of these. At the Arvon Foundation Ltd in Devon there are intensive residential writing courses. Disabled people are welcome, and a few bursaries are offered.

Friendship circles

There are a number of correspondence circles that have developed informally among disabled people. You may see them mentioned in magazines for disabled people, and sometimes in religious papers. As an example, Wider Horizons, founded in 1959, aims to extend the interests of physically disabled people and those who are lonely or housebound, and to promote friendships and the exchange of information and views. To help achieve these objectives, the organisation produces a printed and illustrated 32-page bi-monthly magazine for members. The magazine includes articles from members, and news about aids and welfare. The organisation also links individual members who wish to exchange letters with others in similar circumstances or with common interests.

Pets

Guide Dogs for the Blind, and Hearing Dogs for the Deaf, have already been mentioned, but apart from those who need the services of such animals, many disabled people enjoy the companionship offered by a pet. If you are not sufficiently fit to keep a cat or a dog, or if your home circumstances are unsuitable, you could perhaps keep caged birds such as budgerigars, or goldfish and tropical fish.

Hospitals have found that patients who may make little attempt to communicate with other people will sometimes respond to a dog or cat. Watching fish swim in tanks is therapeutic, and some hospitals and dentists have installed tropical fish tanks in their waiting rooms.

Organisations such as the Friends of the Dogs' Home, Battersea, and PRO-Dogs, are encouraging members to take their dogs on visits to housebound people. Even if you cannot keep a dog of your own, you may enjoy making friends with one that belongs to a neighbour.

Watching birds can be a great interest and delight. Encourage them to come into your garden by providing food and water for them. Spend time looking at them carefully, and notice their fascinating behaviour and habits. You could keep a book on birds to hand.

Chapter 13
Conclusion

As readers will have discovered from this book, there are many disabled people who have been successful in their search for employment. It takes determination and courage to go on looking for jobs when rejections are common and opportunities seem limited, but many do persevere and eventually they find work.

At a time when the MSC forecast that the number of long-term unemployed (people out of work for more than three years) will continue to grow, people with disabilities could feel discouraged. But there are some encouraging signs. There is now greater awareness of the value of disabled workers, and positive steps (such as Lambeth's recent campaign to recruit disabled people for all current vacancies) are being taken.

In the 1986 MSC report, *Corporate Plan*, Mr Bryan Nicholson, MSC Chairman, pointed out that change in industrial structure and technology will continue to create more openings in professional, managerial and technical occupations than in unskilled manual and traditional craft occupations. This means that young people with disabilities who have opportunities of using IT and learning by IT in school will be able to do jobs created through new technology. Some examples of youngsters' achievements are given in *What Sort of Life* by Patricia Rowan.

Here is another encouraging life story. Jane has had cerebral palsy from birth. Her disability left her with speech, hearing, and writing handicaps. She attended Queen Elizabeth's Training College, Leatherhead, to study bookkeeping and accountancy. After completing the course, she worked for a short time in the Foundation's accounts department. Later, she obtained a distinction in OND Business Studies, and also gained a BCom Honours degree at Birmingham University.

After graduating, Jane wrote to ten firms in Birmingham, but she was unsuccessful in obtaining a job. Then Opportunities for the Disabled came to her help, and she is now working with IBM in their Tax Department.

In an interview for *Accountancy* magazine, Jane said: 'Firms are not going to be bothered with handicapped people, when they have a queue of able-bodied people to choose from. You've got to be honest about the problems, but at the same time you've got to show that you are willing and determined to do the work as well as the next person.'

But if all people with disabilities who want to use some of their skills, gifts and time in employment are to be given the chance to do this, everyone in the community must do his or her share.

Employers can give people with disabilities the opportunity of doing a job commensurate with their capabilities. If you are an employer, could you make a positive effort to find a disabled person to fill your next vacancy? Perhaps you could make any adjustments necessary to help him or her to do the job safely, efficiently and comfortably. Giving a person with disabilities the opportunity to work can bring benefits all round: 'Disabled workers are reliable workers' is the experience of many.

Those who advise people with disabilities, or work with them in any sphere, could be constantly alert to possibilities of employment — beyond the traditional openings and schemes. Imaginative, observant friends or advisers, quick to pass on news of new projects and possible vacancies, can be of service to anyone with disabilities, especially those with few contacts, restricted mobility, and little hope that they will find a job.

At the Children's Society Shoebury Family Centre, the project leader sees finding jobs for local youngsters with 'twilight' handicaps as part of his neighbourhood service. He says this entails spending many hours with employers and a little time with members of existing work forces — but he has had some successes, finding jobs as storekeepers, messengers and shelf-fillers for youngsters with epilepsy, mild mental handicaps, poor physical health because of kidney disease in one case, and one who is autistic.

Parents can orientate youngsters towards the world of work and do all in their power to help them prepare for employment — even if this means allowing them to go away from home for training and growth in independence. It is most important to look at *all* the opportunities for unemployed youngsters, not only those intended for youngsters with disabilities.

According to a report by Peter Rummer of the MSC's Youth Training Directorate, only a 'small number' of bodies mention that they are equal opportunities employers when advertising vacancies available through the Youth Training Scheme, yet some of these vacancies would be suitable for young people with physical handicaps.

Anyone with disabilities, who has taken the trouble to study this book, is likely to be keen to work. I hope it has given those readers some new ideas and that they will soon find employment that is satisfying, rewarding and enjoyable.

If you are a person with disabilities and you are successful in your job-search, perhaps you could give another disabled person the benefit of your advice and experience. There are many people who are keen that those with disabilities should have plenty of opportunities for worthwhile employment.

If we all give time and thought to the situation, share our knowledge and take action where it is within our power, those who wish to work will have more chance and choice of employment. In all the schemes and campaigns, projects and organisations, so often it is an individual's concern and action that finally brings success.

Through no fault of their own, many disabled people face life with little prospect of paid employment. If this is your position, don't easily give up seeking possibilities of employment. But, remember, a person ought never to be valued simply in terms of the job he or she does. Life is more than paid employment. Disabled or not, the important thing is to make the most of the time, abilities, and qualities you have.

Perhaps your career will be living courageously and creatively in the situation in which you find yourself, whether or not you have a paid job. For the sake of your family and friends, for the sake of the community, and for your own sake, make the very best that you can of the one life you have.

A cheerful story to end with: when a pupil with 11 O levels — 10 at grade A and one at grade B — then goes on to collect four A levels at grade A, we think he has done well. But this pupil, 19 year old Guy Whitehouse from Crewe, was at Worcester College for the Blind. He is totally blind and had to do all his work in braille. He is now at Balliol College, Oxford.

Appendix to Chapter 13

Facts and figures

During the year 1985-6:

- 77,000 disabled people were placed in work or on to Community Programmes.
- Some 13,400 disabled people attended courses at rehabilitation centres.
- During 1985-86, £19.9 million was spent on the employment rehabilitation programme.
- A new scheme, Employment Initiatives for Disabled People, was introduced to encourage voluntary organisations — by providing financial support — to develop innovative employment services which would complement existing MSC services.
- 3000 severely disabled people were placed into sheltered employment.

(Source: MSC Annual Report, published 14 August 1986)

Commission of the European Communities' document on
Disabled People and Their Employment

This report, produced in 1985, discussed the 'problem', the dimension of the disabled population, the policy and action needed. It includes a number of recommendations which most of us would endorse. It is hoped that they will be adopted by the UK and other member countries.

The following is a selection of quotes from recommendations made in the report:

'Equal opportunities in employment means the preparation of the disabled for "career" jobs through guidance and vocational training. Discrimination which pushes them into occupations where they have no prospects to develop their residual abilities should be avoided.'

'We have to ensure that disabled people are not exploited and that they receive the appropriate wage in both open and sheltered employment and day centres. This wage must permit them a decent way of life at the prevailing social and cultural criteria.'

'Sheltered employment and day centres ought not to be considered as a goal in themselves . . .'

'The disabled person, whether an adult or a child, should follow normal training or education in an ordinary environment wherever possible.'

'Experience demonstrates that disabled persons themselves with appropriate training make excellent rehabilitation workers to support the rehabilitation of other disabled people. This could open very important job opportunities in training centres for disabled workers.'

If you would like to read more you can buy the report at HM Stationery Office or ask if a public library or voluntary organisation library has a copy or will obtain one. It could be worth writing about the report to your representative on the European Parliament. Remember, MPs take far more notice of a number of individual letters than they do when they are sent one letter — even if it is signed by a great many people.

Statement on Disabled Persons Bill from the Royal Association for Disability and Rehabilitation bulletin, January 1986

Disabled Persons (Services, Consultation and Representation) Bill

Tom Clarke's Bill was published on 19 December and presented for second reading in the House of Commons on 17 January. Broadly speaking it updates the Chronically Sick and Disabled Persons' Act 1970 by giving disabled people a much bigger say in the services they need and by moving in three key areas from crisis management to crisis prevention.

Clause 1 gives disabled people the right to appoint representatives to speak for them or accompany them when plans for the services they need are being discussed. The representative (based on the work of organisations such as Advocacy Alliance) will also have the right of access to the disabled person at all reasonable times. Clause 2 builds on Section 2 of the 1970 Act to ensure that all needs are considered in the assessment for any service, that the disabled person has a right to the information on which the assessment is being made unless it is confidential, and should receive a written record of the decision. The most radical changes, however, probably come in Clauses 3 to 7. In three key areas full assessments of disabled people's needs are to be triggered (with their consent) before a crisis has occurred. These areas are: disabled people leaving full-time education, people leaving a mental handicap or psychiatric hospital after six months as an in-patient and people whose carers can no longer cope. Clause 5 allows carers to ask a local authority to determine whether they are capable of undertaking the tasks they are required to do and to determine their need for support and assistance. If they cannot cope, the authority must do a full-scale assessment of the needs of the disabled person. The procedures for these assessments are specified in Clauses 6 and 7 and are modelled on the procedures for making statements of a person's needs in the Education Act 1981. Another key feature of this part of the Act is the right to have an interpreter if the disabled person is unable to communicate with the person assessing his needs on account of his disability or inadequate command of English. Clause 8 extends this part of the Bill to Scotland.

Clause 9 requires authorities providing a service under Section 2 of the 1970 Act to inform the disabled person of services provided by voluntary organisations and other public bodies as well as the Social Services Department. Clause 10 requires bodies co-opting a disabled person to consult organisations of disabled people first. Clause 11 requires statements from the Secretary of State of the numbers of people in mental handicap and psychiatric hospitals and the provisions for people who have been moved into the community in the preceding year. Clause 12 gives disabled people the right to have their needs considered in local authority structure plans. Clause 13 concerns co-operation between health boards and local authorities in Scotland.

In summary, therefore, the Bill does not so much give new rights to services as give disabled people more rights to a say in those services which it is already the duty of authorities to provide. Much money is wasted because authorities do not listen to the real experts — the disabled person and his or her family.

Chapter 14

Useful Addresses

Please enclose a stamped and self-addressed envelope with any requests for information or publications.

National telephone dialling codes are given here, but local codes may differ; please check in your *Code Book* before making a call.

Access Committee for England
35 Great Smith Street, London
SW1P 3BJ; 01-222 7980
Promotes access to buildings and the environment.

Advisory, Conciliation and Arbitration Service (ACAS)
Head Office: 11-12 St James's Square, London SW1Y 4LA; 01-214 6000.
Regional offices are in the phone book.

Air Transport Users Committee
129 Kingsway, London
WC2B 6NN; 01-242 3882

Alder Valley Services
Halimote Road, Aldershot
GU1 3EG

The All Party Disablement Group
Secretary: Fidelity Simpson, Ronshed Farm, Underiver, Sevenoaks, Kent
or c/o RADAR

Amnesty International
1 Easton Street, London
WC1X 8DJ; 01-833 1771

Anything Nostalgic
35 Northcourt Avenue, Reading
RG2 7HE; 0734 871479

Arvon Foundation Ltd
Totleigh Barton, Sheepwash, Devon EX21 5NS

Association for All Speech Impaired Children (AFASIC)
347 Central Markets, Smithfield, London EC1A 9LH; 01-236 3632

The Association for Spina Bifida and Hydrocephalus (ASBAH)
22 Upper Woburn Place, London
WC1H 0EP; 01-388 1382

The Association of Blind Piano Tuners
224 Great Portland Street, London
W1N 6AA

The Association of Disabled Professionals
General Secretary: Mrs Peggy Marchant, The Stables, 73 Pound Road, Banstead, Surrey SM7 2HU; Burgh Heath (073 73) 52366

The Association of Visually Handicapped Office Workers
Secretary: Miss E Siekmann, 14 Verulam House, Hammersmith Grove, London W6

Bank of Scotland
Home Banking Centre, Freepost, Edinburgh EH1 0AA;
031-346 6060

Beaumont College of Further Education
Slyne Road, Lancaster LA2 6AP;
0524 64278

The British Deaf Association
38 Victoria Place, Carlisle
CA1 1HU; 0228 48844

The British Franchise Association
Franchise Chambers, 75a Bell
Street, Henley-on-Thames,
Oxon RG9 2BD; 0491 578049

British Jigsaw Library
Old Homend, Stretton Grandison,
Ledbury, Herefordshire HR8 2TW

**British Limbless Ex-Servicemen's
Association**
Frankland Moore House,
185-187 High Road, Chadwell
Heath, Essex; 01-590 1124

**The British Paraplegic Sports
Society**
Ludwig Guttman Sports Centre,
Harvey Road, Aylesbury,
Buckinghamshire HP21 8PP;
0296 84848

British Polio Fellowship
Bell Close, West End Road, Ruislip,
Middlesex HA4 6LP; Ruislip 75515

**British School of Motoring
Assessment Centre**
81-87 Hartfield Road, London
SW19 3TJ; 01-540 8262

**British Sports Association for the
Disabled**
Hayward House, Barnard Crescent,
Aylesbury, Buckinghamshire
HP21 9PP; 0296 27889

British Talking Book Service,
see National Listening Library

**British Unemployment
Resource Network**
318 Summer Lane, Birmingham
B19 3RL; 021-359 3562

Camphill Village Trust
Delrow House, Aldenham, Watford,
Hertfordshire WD2 8DJ;
Radlett (092 76) 6006

**Central Council for Education
and Training in Social Work**
Derbyshire House, St Chad Street,
London WC1H 8AD; 01-278 2455.
Regional offices in Belfast, Cardiff
and Edinburgh.

**The Central Register and Clearing
House**
3 Crawford Place, London
W1H 2BN. For information leaflet
giving details of all degree and
other advanced courses within the
Central Register and Clearing House
Scheme, ie courses other than
university degree courses, eg
education colleges.

**The Centre for Deaf and Speech
Therapy**
Keeley House, Keeley Street,
London WC2B 4BA; 01-430 0548

**Centre on Environment for the
Handicapped**
126 Albert Street, London
NW1 7NF; 01-482 2247

CFL Vision
Chalfont Grove, Gerrards Cross,
Buckinghamshire SL9 8TN;
Chalfont St Giles (02407) 4433

The Children's Society,
see Church of England Children's
Society

**Church of England Children's
Society**
(known as The Children's Society),
Edward Rudolf House,
69-85 Margery Street, London
WC1X 0JL; 01-837 4299

Citizens' Advice Bureau (CAB)
Myddelton House,
115-123 Pentonville Road, London
N1 9LZ; 01-833 2181.
Local offices are in the phone book.

The Civil Service Commission
Alencon Link, Basingstoke,
Hampshire RG21 1JB; 0256 29222

The College of Speech Therapists
Harold Poster House, 6 Lechmere
Road, London NW2 5BU;
01-459 8521

Commission for Racial Equality
Elliott House, 10-12 Allington
Street, London SW1E 5EH;
01-828 7022

**Committee on Mobility for
Scotland**
Princes House, 5 Shandwick Place,
Edinburgh EH2 4RG;
031-229 8632

Communication Aids Centres
Visitors should always contact a
Centre before visiting as an
appointment is usually necessary.

Aids Centre, Rehabilitation
Engineering Unit, Musgrave Park
Hospital, Stockman's Lane, *Belfast*
BT9 7JB; 0232 669501

Disabled Living Centre, Broadgate
House, 260 Broad Street,
Birmingham B1 2HF;
021-643 0980

Aids Centre, 8 Queens Street,
Blackpool FY1 1PD; 0253 21084

Frenchay Hospital, Frenchay,
Bristol BS16 1LE;
0272 565656 ext 204.
Contact Mrs Easton.

Aids and Information Centre,
Wales Council for the Disabled,
Caerbrady Industrial Estate,
Bedwas Road, *Caerphilly*
CF8 3SL; 0222 887325

Rookwood Hospital, Llandaff
Road, *Cardiff*, South Glamorgan
CF5 2YN; 0222 566281.
Contact Mrs Binks.

South Lothian Aids Distribution
and Exhibiton Centre, Astley
Ainslie Hospital, *Edinburgh*
EH9 2HL; 031-447 9200

CALL Centre (Communication
Aids for Learners in Lothian),
University of Edinburgh,
4 Buccleuch Place, *Edinburgh*
EH8 9JT; 031-667 1438

Royal National Institute for the
Deaf, 9a Clairmont Gardens,
Glasgow 3; 041-332 0343

The William Merritt Aids and
Information Centre for Disabled
People, St Mary's Hospital,
Greenhill Road, Armley, *Leeds*
LS12 3QE; 0532 793140

Trent Region Aids Information,
76 Clarendon Park Road,
Leicester LE2 3AD;
0533 700747

Merseyside Aids Centre, Youens
Way, East Prescott Road, *Liverpool*
L14 2EP; 051-228 9221

Charing Cross Hospital, Fulham
Palace Road, *London* W6 8RF;
01-748 2040 ext 3064.
Contact Miss Le Patourel.

Disabled Living Foundation,
Aids Centre, 380-384 Harrow
Road, *London* W9 2HU;
01-289 6111

Institute of Child Health,
The Wolfson Centre, Mecklenburgh
Square, *London* WC1N 2AP;
01-837 7618.
Contact Mrs Jolleff.

Royal National Institute for the
Deaf, 105 Gower Street, *London*
WC1E 6AH; 01-387 8033

Disabled Living Centre CHS,
Redbank House, 43 Redbank,
Manchester M4 4HF;
061-832 3678

Newcastle Upon Tyne Council
for the Disabled Aids Centre, The
Dene Centre, Castle Farm Road,
Newcastle upon Tyne NE3 1PH;
091-284 0480

Special Unit for the Hearing
Impaired, Civic Centre, Barras
Bridge, *Newcastle upon Tyne*;
0632 328520 ext 63

Disabled Living Centre, Prince
Albert Road, Eastney,
Portsmouth; 0705 737174

Southampton Aids Centre,
Southampton General Hospital,
Tremona Road, *Southampton*
SO9 4XY; 0703 777222 ext
3414 or 3233

Sheffield Aids Centre, Family and Community Services, 87-89 The Wicker, *Sheffield* S3 8HT; 0742 737025

Stockport Aids Centre, St Thomas Hospital, 59a Shaw Heath, *Stockport* SK3 8BL; 061-480 7201

Boulton Road, *West Bromwich*, West Midlands B70 9NR; 021-553 0908. Contact Mrs Robinson.

The following exhibitions tour the country. The itinerary will be supplied on request. No appointment is necessary.

Mobile Aids Centre, Scottish Council on Disability, Princes House, 5 Shandwick Place, *Edinburgh* EH2 4RG; 031-229 8632

Visiting Aids Centre, The Spastics Society, 16 Fitzroy Square, *London* W1P 5HQ; 01-387 9571

Coombe Herbs
1 Beaumont Cottages, Gittisham, Nr Honiton, Devon EX14 0AG

The Co-operative College
Stanford Hall, Loughborough, Leicestershire LE12 5QR; 0509 822333

Co-operative Development Agency
Broadmead House, 21 Panton Street, London SW1Y 4DR; 01-839 2988

Council for National Academic Awards
The Publications Officer, 344 Gray's Inn Road, London WC1X 8BP; 01-278 4411

Council for Small Industries in Rural Areas (CoSIRA)
141 Castle Street, Salisbury, Wiltshire SP1 3PT; 0722 336255. Regional offices are in the phone book.

Council for the Accreditation of Correspondence Colleges
27 Marylebone Road, London NW1 5JS; 01-935 5391

CRAC Publications
Hobsons Ltd, Bateman Street, Cambridge CB2 1LZ; 0223 354551

The Crafts Council
12 Waterloo Place, London SW1Y 4AU; 01-837 1917

The Department of Education and Science
Room 2/11, Elizabeth House, York Road, London SE1 7PH; 01-934 9000

Department of the Environment
2 Marsham Street, London SW1P 3EB; 01-212 3434

Department of Health and Social Security
DHSS Leaflets Unit, PO Box 21, Stanmore, Middlesex HA7 1AY

Department of Transport
Door-to-Door Guide, Victoria Street, South Ruislip, Middlesex HA4 ON2; 01-212 4431 or 3547

Derby Disabled Driving Centre
Derwent Hospital, Derby DE2 4BB; 0332 47141

Derwen Training College for the Disabled
Oswestry, Salop SY11 3JA; 0691 661234. Voluntary body with board of governors.

The Design Centre/Council
28 Haymarket, London SW1Y 4SU; 01-839 8000

Disabled Drivers' Association
18 Creekside, Deptford, London SE8 3DZ; 01-692 7141

The Disabled Drivers' Motor Club Ltd
1a Dudley Gardens, London W13 9LU; 01-840 1515

DDMC
Membership Bureau, Freepost, Coventry CV2 3BR

Disabled Graduates Data Bank
Careers Advisory Service
University of Nottingham, University Park, Nottingham NG7 2RD; 0602 506101

Disabled Living Foundation
380-384 Harrow Road, London
W9 2HU; 01-239 6111

Disability Alliance Educational and Research Association
25 Denmark Street, London
WC2H 8NJ; 01-240 0806

Disablement Incomes Group
Attlee House, Commercial Street,
London E1 6LR; 01-247 2128

Disablement Information and Advice Line called DIAL UK
Victoria Buildings, 117 High Street,
Clay Cross, Chesterfield S45 9DZ;
0246 864498 (Monday-Friday
9-5). A call to this number will
supply the number for the nearest
of the 75 branches.

Jennie and Bob Donaldson
Gorslwyd Farm, TanYGroes,
Cardigan, Dyfed SA43 2HZ;
0239 810593

Dr Barnado's
Tanners Lane, Barkingside,
Essex; 01-550 8822

Educational Guidance Services for Adults
ECCTIS; PO Box 88, Walton Hall,
Milton Keynes MK7 6DB. Write for
a list to this address and mark the
letter for the attention of
Miss Tracy Vardy.

Enham Village Centre
The Secretary, The White House,
Enham-Alamein, Nr Andover,
Hampshire SP11 6HJ

EP Training Services Ltd
6a High Street, Esher, Surrey
KT10 9RT

Equal Opportunities Commission
Overseas House, Quay Street,
Manchester M3 3HN; 061-833 9244

Full-Employ (Project Full-Employ)
102 Park Village East, London
NW1 3SP; 01-387 1222. Ask for
address of your nearest local
project.

Finchale Training College
Durham DH1 5RX; 0385 62634

Fircroft College
Bristol Road, Selly Oak,
Birmingham B29 6LH;
021-472 0116

The French Government Tourist Office
178 Piccadilly, London W1V 0AL;
01-499 6911 or 7622

Gardens for the Disabled Trust
Little Dane, Biddenden, Kent;
0580 291214

The General Synod Board of Education
Church House, Westminster,
London SW1P 3NZ

The Grange School of Stitchery and Lace
Rectory Lane, Bookham, Surrey;
0372 526 081. This school is a
private registered charity. Students
need to have an aptitude for
needlework.

The Greater London Association for Disabled People (GLAD)
336 Brixton Road, London
SW9 7AA; 01-274 0107

John Grooms Association for the Disabled
10 Gloucester Drive, London
N4 2LP; 01-802 7272

The Groupwork Centre
21a Kingsland High Street, London
E8 2JS; 01-254 9753

Guide Dogs for the Blind Association
9-11 Park Street, Windsor,
Berkshire; 075 35 55711

Handicapped Persons Research Unit
Newcastle upon Tyne Polytechnic,
Coach Lane Campus, Newcastle
upon Tyne NE7 7TW; 091-232 6002

Haven Christian Training Centre
1 Westgate Hill, Pembroke, Dyfed;
0646 685469

Hearing Dogs for the Deaf
Little Close, Lower Ickneild Way,
Lewknor, Oxon OX9 5RY;
0844 53898

Hereward College
Bramston Crescent, Tile Hill Lane,
Coventry CV4 9SW; 0203 461231

Hillcroft College
South Bank, Surbiton, Surrey
KT6 6DF; 01-399 2688

Holiday Care Service
2 Old Bank Chambers, Station
Road, Horley, Surrey RH6 9HW;
0293 774535

Institute of Advanced Motorists
IAM House, 359-365 Chiswick
High Road, London W4 4HS;
01-994 4403

IT World Ltd
Asphalte House, Palace Street,
London SW1E 5HS

Joint Aid Centres Council
76 Clarendon Park Road, Leicester
LE2 3AD; 0533 70074. For address
of your nearest Aids Centre.

**Joint Committee on Mobility for
the Disabled**
9 Moss Close, Pinner, Middlesex
HA5 3AY; 01-866 7884

Jubilee Trust
8 Bedford Row, London
WC1R 4BY; 01-430 0524

King's Fund Centre
126 Albert Street, London
NW1 7NF; 01-267 6111

Learning to Drive Centre
The Government's Transport and
Road Research Laboratory, Old
Wokingham Road, Crowthorne,
Berkshire RG11 6AU;
0344 779014

Livewire
Freepost, Belfast BT7 1BR
Freepost, Cambridge CB2 1BR
Freepost, Newton Mearns, Glasgow
G77 5BR

London College of Furniture
41-47 Commercial Road, London
E1 1LA; 01-247 1953

London Regional Transport, see
LRT Unit for Disabled Passengers

Lord Mayor Treloar College
Holybourne, Alton, Hampshire;
0420 83508

LRT Unit for Disabled Passengers
55 Broadway, London SW1H 0BD;
01-222 1234

Manpower Services Commission
Moorfoot, Sheffield S1 4PQ;
0742 753275
5 Kirk Loan, Corstorphine,
Edinburgh EH12 7HD;
031-334 9821

*Careers and Occupational
Information Centre*
Sales Department, Room W1101,
Moorfoot, Sheffield S1 4PQ

*Professional and Executive
Recruitment Division*
2 Fitzwilliam Gate, Sheffield
S1 4JH; 0742 704585

MENCAP
123 Golden Lane, London
EC1Y 0RT; 01-253 9433

*Mencap Pathway Employment
Service*
169a City Road, Cardiff CF2 3JB

Millfield Village of Education
Street, Somerset BA16 0YD

Mind (National Association for
Mental Health)
22 Harley Street, London
W1N 2ED; 01-637 0741

Morley College
61 Westminster Bridge Road,
London SE1 7PB; 01-928 8501/
633 0053

Motability
Boundary House, 91-93
Charterhouse Street, London
EC1M 6BT; 01-253 1211

The Muscular Dystrophy Group
Nattrass House, 35 Macaulay Road,
London SW4 0QP; 01-270 8055

**National Advisory Centre on
Careers for Women**
Drayton House, 30 Gordon Street,
London WC1H 0AX; 01-380 0117

**National Association for the
Welfare of Children in Hospital**
Argyle House, Euston Road,
London NW1 2SD; 01-833 2041

**The National Bureau for
Handicapped Students**
336 Brixton Road, London
SW9 7AA; 01-274 0565

National Bus Company
172 Buckingham Palace Road,
London SW1W 9PN; 01-730 3453

National Children's Home
85 Highbury Park, London N5 1UD;
01-226 2033

National Computing Centre
Bracken House, Charles Street,
Manchester M1 7BD; 061-273 5173.
Base for the Threshold Scheme.
Oxford Road, Manchester M1 7ED;
061-278 6333. General
information on courses.

National Elfrida Rathbone Society
11a Whitworth Street, Manchester
M1 3GW; 061-236 5358

The National Extension College
18 Brooklands Avenue, Cambridge
CB2 2HN; 0223 63465

**National League of the Blind and
Disabled**
2 Tenterden Road, London
N17 8BE; 01-808 6030

National Listening Library
12 Lant Street, London SE1 1QR;
01-407 9417

National Mobility Centre
MOTEC, High Ercall, Telford,
Salop TF6 6RB; 0952 770881

**National Newspaper and Magazine
Tape Service for the Blind**
68a High Street, Heathfield, East
Sussex TN21 8JB; 04352 6102

National Society for Epilepsy
Chalfont Centre for Epilepsy,
Chalfont St Peter, Buckinghamshire SL9 0RJ; Chalfont St Giles
(024 27) 3991

**National Star Centre for Disabled
Youth**
Ullenwood Manor, Cheltenham,
Gloucestershire GL53 9RH;
0242 2763

Newbattle Abbey
Dalkeith, Midlothian, Scotland
EH22 3IC; 031-663 1921

New Hope Bible College
Faith Acres, Peterhead, Scotland
AB4 7DQ; 0779 83 251

**Northern Ireland Council for
the Handicapped**
2 Annandale Avenue, Belfast
BT7 3JR; 0232 640011

**North London School of
Physiotherapy for the Visually
Handicapped**
10 Highgate Hill, London N19;
01-272 1659

Open BTEC
Berkshire House, 168-173 High
Holborn, London WC1V 7AG;
01-379 7970

The Open University
PO Box 48, Milton Keynes
MK7 6AB

Associate Student Programme
PO Box 76, The Open University,
Walton Hall, Milton Keynes
MK7 6AN

Opportunities for the Disabled
London Headquarters, 1 Bank
Buildings, Princes Street, London
EC2R 8EU; 01-726 4961

Oxford Polytechnic
Cartography Department,
Headington, Oxford OX3 0BP;
0865 64777

Papworth Village Settlement
The Secretary, Papworth Everard,
Nr Cambridge, Cambridgeshire
CB3 8RF; 0480 830341

The Parkinson's Disease Society
36 Portland Place, London
W1N 3DG; 01-323 1174

**Physically Handicapped and
Able-Bodied (PHAB)**
Tavistock House North, Tavistock
Square, London WC1H 9HX;
01-388 1963

**Polytechnics Central Admissions
System**
PO Box 67, Cheltenham,
Gloucestershire GL50 3AP

Portland Training College
Harlow Wood, Nottingham Road,
Mansfield, Nottingham NG18 4TJ;
Blidworth 2141

Practical Action
Victoria Chambers, 16-20 Strutton
Ground, London SW1P 2HP;
01-225 3351

The Prince's Trust
6 Bedford Row, London
WC1R 4BU; 01-430 0524

PRO-Dogs
4 New Road, Ditton, Maidstone,
Kent; West Malling (0732) 848499

**Production Engineering Research
Association (PERA)**
Occupational Aids Project,
Nottingham Road, Melton
Mowbray, Leicestershire;
0664 64133 ext 362

**Professional and Executive
Recruitment (PER)**
Head Office, Fitzwilliam House,
Fitzwilliam Gate, Sheffield S1 4JH;
0742 704585. Local offices are in
the phone book.

Project Full-Employ
Robert Hyde House, 48 Bryanston
Square, London W1H 7LN;
01-262 2405. Contact for address
of nearest project of the 21 in
England and Scotland.

**Psychiatric Rehabilitation
Association**
The Groupwork Centre, 21a
Kingsland High Street, London
E8 2JS; 01-254 9753

**Queen Elizabeth's Foundation for
the Disabled**
Leatherhead, Surrey KT22 0BN;
Oxshott (037 284) 2204

Queen Elizabeth's Training College
Leatherhead, Surrey KT22 0BN;
Oxshott (037 284) 2204

RADAR, see Royal Association for
Disability and Rehabilitation

**Rehabilitation Engineering
Movement Advisory Panels
(REMAP)**
25 Mortimer Street, London
W1N 8AB; 01-637 5400

Remploy Ltd
415 Edgware Road, London
NW2 6LR; 01-452 8020

Riding for the Disabled Association
National Agricultural Centre,
Kenilworth, Warwickshire
CV8 2LY; Coventry (0203) 56107

**Royal Association in Aid of the
Deaf and the Dumb (RADD)**
27 Old Oak Road, London W3 7HN;
01-743 6187

**Royal Association for Disability
and Rehabilitation (RADAR)**
25 Mortimer Street, London
W1N 8AB; 01-637 5400

The Royal British Legion
48 Pall Mall, London SW1Y 5JY;
01-930 8131

Royal British Legion Industries
Preston Hall, Maidstone, Kent
ME20 7NL; 0622 77202

Royal Horticultural Society
Wisley, Ripley, Surrey;
0483 225329

**The Royal National Institute for
the Blind**
224 Great Portland Street, London
W1N 6AA; 01-388 1266

Rehabilitation Centre
Manor House, Middle Lincombe
Road, Torquay, Devon TG1 2NG;
0803 214523

Training College
5 Pembridge Place, London
W2 4XB; 01-229 6673

**Royal National Institute for the
Deaf**
105 Gower Street, London
WC1E 6AH; 01-387 8033

**The Royal Society for Mentally
Handicapped Children and Adults,**
see MENCAP

**St Loye's College for Training the
Disabled for Commerce and
Industry**
Fairfield House, Topsham Road,
Exeter EX2 6EP; 0392 55428

**Scottish Branch of the British
Red Cross**
Alexandra House, 204 Bath Street,
Glasgow G2 48L; 041-332 9591

The Scottish Council on Disability
Princes House, 5 Shandwick Place,
Edinburgh EH2 4RG;
031-229 8632

Scottish Education Department
43 Jeffrey Street, Edinburgh
EH1 1DN; 031-445 8400

Scottish Sports Association,
contact British Sports Association

The Shaftesbury Society
2a Amity Grove, London
SW20 0LJ; 01-846 6655

SHAPE
1 Thorpe Close, London W10 5XL;
01-960 9245

Sherrards Training Centre
Digswell Hill, Welwyn,
Hertfordshire AL6 9AW;
07073 35231

Sisters Against Disability
Flat 7, 94 Park Road, Beckenham,
Kent BR3 1QT

Sisters of Jesus Crucified
The Guest Mistress, St John's
Priory, Castle Cary, Somerset
BA7 7PF

The Small Firms Service
Phone operator on 100 and ask
for Freefone Enterprise

The Spastics Society
12 Park Crescent, London
W1N 4EQ; 01-636 5020

The Spinal Injuries Association
(SIA)
Yeoman House, 76 St James's
Lane, London N10 3DF;
01-444 2121

Tandata Marketing Limited
Malvern, Worcestershire

Training Workshops Resource Unit
60 Highbury Grove, London
N5 2AG; 01-359 1363

Trades Union Congress
Congress House, Great Russell
Street, London WC1B 3LS;
01-636 4030

Treloar Trust
Froyle, Alton, Hampshire;
Bentley (0420) 22442

The Universities Central Council
on Admissions
PO Box 28, Cheltenham,
Gloucestershire GL50 1HY

Village Centres Association
Enham Village Centre, The
White House, Enham-Alamein,
Nr Andover, Hampshire SP11 6HJ.
Papworth Village Settlement,
Cambridgeshire

The Volunteer Centre
29 Lower Kings Road,
Berkhamsted, Hertfordshire;
04427 73311

Wales Council for the Disabled
Caerbragdy Industrial Estate,
Bedwas Road, Caerphilly, Mid
Glamorgan CF8 3SL; 0222 887325

Welsh Sports Association, contact
British Sports Association

West Dean College
The Principal: Peter Sarginson,
Chichester, Sussex PO18 0QZ;
Singleton (0243 63) 301

Westminster Association for Mental
Health
Church House, Newton Road,
London W2 5LS; 01-221 6198

Winged Fellowship Trust
Angel House, Pentonville Road,
London N1 9XD; 01-833 2594.
Provides holidays for severely
disabled people.

Wider Horizons
Mrs M Fletcher, Westbrook, Back
Lane, Malvern, Worcestershire
WR14 2HJ

Young Enterprise
Robert Hyde House, 48 Bryanston
Square, London W1H 7LN;
01-262 2405. For self-employment
advice.

Youth Enterprise Scheme (YES)
16-20 Strutton Ground, London
SW1P 2HP; 01-222 3341

Chapter 15

Further Reading

The following titles are a selection only; many of them are mentioned in the text. Try to ensure that you have found the latest edition — leaflets in particular are frequently updated.

If you are ordering a book by post, check the correct amount beforehand with the organisation concerned and enclose payment with the order; this will save writing extra letters if prices have increased.

Chapter 1. Making a Choice — to Work or Not to Work

Executive Job-hunting for People with Health Problems or Disability,
  Professional and Executive Recruitment
'Industrial Injuries: Disablement Benefit and Increases', NI6 (April 1983,
  revised November 1985)
'Making Our Way', The Association for Spina Bifida and Hydrocephalus,
  1984.

Chapter 2. Employment for People with Disabilities

A Better Deal for the Disabled, General and Municipal Workers Union,
  1981
'Code of Good Practice on the Employment of Disabled People', Manpower
  Services Commission
'The Disabled Persons (Employment) Acts 1944 and 1958', DPL 2,
  Manpower Services Commission
'The Disabled Persons Register', DPL 1, Manpower Services Commission
Employers' Guide to Disabilities, Bert Massie and Melvyn Kettle, RADAR
  (£5)
'Employing Disabled People — Sources of Help', EPL 147 (February 1985),
  Manpower Services Commission
'Employing Someone with Epilepsy', EPL 40, Manpower Services
  Commission
'Equal Pay for Work of Equal Value', Equal Opportunities Commission,
  1984
'Help for Handicapped People', HB1, HB1(S), DHSS
'Making Our Way', The Association for Spina Bifida and Hydrocephalus,
  1984
A Right to Work — Disability and Employment, Susan Lonsdale and
  Alan Walker, Disability Alliance, 1984 (£2)

'TUC Guide on the Employment of Disabled People', Trades Union Congress. (35p plus 20p postage and packing)

Chapter 3. The Disabled School-Leaver

Directory of Opportunities for School-Leavers with Disabilities, Queen Elizabeth's Foundation for the Disabled, 1985. (£4 including postage and packing. An optional alphabetical index costs an extra 75p.)

Disabled People and Their Employment, EEC, 1985

Executive Post, Professional and Executive Recruitment

'An Ordinary Working Life, vocational services for people with mental handicap', King's Fund Centre, 1984

'Working It Out, an aid to deciding about jobs', Manpower Services Commission

Chapter 4. Looking for Advice on Careers and Employment

'Thinking about Training', ATL 49, Manpower Services Commission

Employment News, Department of Employment

'Executive Job-hunting for people with health problems or disability', Professional and Executive Recruitment

Executive Post, Professional and Executive Recruitment

'Getting Back to Work', Manpower Services Commission

Graduate Post, Professional and Executive Recruitment

Jobhunting pack, Manpower Services Commission

Running Your Own Driving School, Nigel Stacey, Kogan Page, 1984

Chapter 5. Education and Training Opportunities

The Advocate, journal of the National League of the Blind and Disabled

Directory of Grant Making Trusts, Charities Aid Foundation

Directory of London Training Workshops 1985-86, Training Workshops Research Unit

'Grants to Students', Department of Education and Science

The Grants Register 1987-89, Macmillan, 1986

'Mature Students and Universities', The Universities Central Council on Admissions

'Residential Training Opportunities for Disabled People', TSD N 278, Manpower Services Commission

Soundbarrier, journal of the Royal National Institute for the Deaf

'Training Opportunities for Disabled People', TSD N 121, Manpower Services Commission

UCCA Handbook, How to apply for admission to a university, The Universities Central Council on Admissions

Chapter 6. Sheltered Employment and Rehabilitation

Directory of Opportunities for School-Leavers with Disabilities. See entry under Chapter 3 above.

Chapter 7. Looking at Careers

An A-Z of Careers and Jobs, 2nd edition, Kogan Page, 1986
'Design Courses in Britain, Design Council
Directory for Disabled People, A Darnbrough and D Kinrade, Woodhead-Faulkner in association with RADAR, 4th edition, 1985 (£11.50; £12.50 from RADAR including postage and packing)
'Job Outlines', Manpower Services Commission
Kogan Page Careers Series: 69 titles, each on a separate career area; send for leaflet
Occupations, Manpower Services Commission, annual (£15)

Chapter 8. Running Your Own Business

Executive Post, Professional and Executive Recruitment
'How to Make Your Business Grow', Small Firms Service
'Signposts to Self-Employment', Project Full-Employ (£1.95 from the Self-Employment Resource Centre, 31 Clerkenwell Close, London EC1R 0AT; 01-251 6037)

The following books on self-employment and small business are a selection published by Kogan Page; * denotes a *Daily Telegraph* guide.
Buying a Shop, 3rd edition, 1986, A St J Price
Computers Mean Business, 1984, Jacquetta Megarry
Financial Management for the Small Business,* 1984, Colin Barrow
Getting Sales, 1984, Richard D Smith and Ginger Dick
Guardian Guide to Running a Small Business, 5th edition, 1986, edited by Clive Woodcock
How to Buy a Business,* 1983, Peter Farrell
How to Choose Business Premises, 1986, Howard Green, Brian Chalkley and Paul Foley
Law for the Small Business,* 4th edition, 1985, Patricia Clayton
Running Your Own Shop, 1985, Roger Cox
The Small Business Action Kit, 1986, John Rosthorn, Andrew Haldane, Edward Blackwell and John Wholey
Starting a Successful Small Business, 1985, M J Morris
Successful Marketing for the Small Business,* 1985, Dave Patten
Taking up a Franchise,* 3rd edition, 1986, Godfrey Golzen and Colin Barrow
Working for Yourself,* 8th edition, 1986, Godfrey Golzen
Writing for a Living, 1985, Ian Linton

Chapter 9. Information Technology

Computer Help for the Disabled, L Ridgway and S McKears, Souvenir Press, 1985
Directory of Opportunities in New Technology, Kogan Page, annual
Information Technology and Further Education, Brieda Vincent and Tom Vincent, Kogan Page, 1985 (includes a chapter on disabled students)
Living Independently, Ann Shearer, Centre on Environment for the Handicapped and King Edward's Hospital Fund for London, 1982

New Information Technology in the Education of Disabled Children and Adults, T Vincent, D Hawkridge and G Hales, Croom Helm, 1984
'New Outlook', Manpower Services Commission
'Working with Computers', Royal National Institute for the Blind

Chapter 10. Equipment for Living

'British Telecom Guide to Equipment and Services for Disabled Customers' (Chapters include Notes for Hearing Aid Users; Notes for People with Speech Difficulties; Visual Handicap; Mobility Impairment; Mental Handicap; Telephones in Public Places; and Emergency Call Systems. There are also useful addresses.)
Directory for Disabled People. See entry under Chapter 7 above.
Link, The Association for Spina Bifida and Hydrocephalus magazine
'Making Our Way', The Association for Spina Bifida and Hydrocephalus, 1984
Voluntary Organisations, National Council of Voluntary Organisations (a directory)
'Without Words', The College of Speech Therapists

Chapter 11. Mobility

'Access to the Underground', London Regional Transport (70p)
Door-to-Door, Department of Transport (a free guide to transport for disabled people), 2nd edition, 1986
'Help for Handicapped People', HB1 and HB1(S), DIISS
'Making Our Way', The Association for Spina Bifida and Hydrocephalus, 1984
'Mobility Allowance for people unable or virtually unable to walk', NI 211, DHSS

Chapter 12. Using Your Spare Time Creatively

Activity and Hobby Holidays, English Tourist Board
'British Rail and Disabled Travellers', British Rail
'Contact', RADAR magazine, quarterly
Directory for Disabled People, See entry under Chapter 7 above.
Disabled Driver, magazine
Disabled People and Their Employment, EEC document
England's Seaside, English Tourist Board
Farm Holidays, English Tourist Board
Guide for the Disabled Traveller, Automobile Association
Handicapped Living (now called *Caring,* A E Morgan, Stanley House, 9 West Street, Epsom, Surrey KT18 7RL)
Holidays for Disabled People, RADAR
New Society, weekly journal
Travelling with British Rail — a Guide for Disabled People (£2.50 from RADAR)
'Voluntary Work and Social Security Benefits', DHSS
'Who Looks After You', British Airports Authority
The Writers' and Artists' Year Book, A & C Black, annual
Writing for a Living, Ian Linton, Kogan Page, 1985

Index